To Stacy Cole,
My brother in the
struggle ... you
can make a difference!

Roland
7/93

THE GHETTO SOLUTION

the Ghetto Solution

ROLAND GILBERT
CHEO TYEHIMBA-TAYLOR

WRS
PUBLISHING

A Division of WRS Group, Inc.
Waco, Texas

First published in the United States of America in 1994 by WRS Publishing,
A Division of WRS Group, Inc., 701 N. New Road, Waco, Texas 76710
Book design by Kenneth Turbeville
Jacket design by Joe James

10 9 8 7 6 5 4 3 2

Library of Congress Cataloging-in-Publication Data

Gilbert, Roland, 1947-
        The ghetto solution / Roland Gilbert, Cheo Tyehimba-Taylor.
                p.   cm.
        ISBN 1-56796-021-9 : $19.95
        1. Gilbert, Roland, 1947--   . 2. Afro-Americans--Biography. 3.
Simba, Inc. 4. Afro-Americans--Life skills guides. 5. Afro-Americans--
Social conditions--1975-
6. Afro-Americans--Psychology.
I. Tyehimba-Taylor, Cheo, 1964--   II. Title.
E185.97.G52A3 1994
305.896'073'092--dc20
                                                        93-38867
                                                        CIP

Dedication

I *dedicate this book to my wife Alyce, who knows everything about me and loves me unconditionally; to my daughter Terry who knows who I am, but not who I was; to my sons Roland and Maurice who know who I was and are learning to know who I am, and to my mother, Mary, who just loves me, and doesn't need or want to know; to my father Maurice, Sr., who I finally learned to know and love; to my sister and brother Rosemary and Maurice, Jr., who are learning to forget who I was and accept who I am; to my second mother Winfrey Ford who sees only the best in me; to my friend for life Carl Harris who survived the ghetto with me; to all of our ghetto children who deserve to be more than we have taught them to be; and to all the Simba Leaders—African American pioneers, and courageous warriors, creating a better future for ourselves and all of America.*

Table Of Contents

Preface

In the following chapters of this book I will show you some excerpts from my life. Hopefully you will understand from this what the only real and lasting ghetto solution is. My life is an example of that solution. That is, no matter what my opportunities or advantages were, I did not overcome the ghetto until I changed the way that I thought, felt, and acted towards myself, my circumstances, and my environment.

I wrote this book to highlight the fact that we need to stop making the same mistakes over and over again in our families, communities, corporations, and government. We keep trying to manipulate external circumstances rather than internal perspectives and keep expecting things to change. This is because no one, not our policy makers, not our funding organizations, not our healthcare institutions know how, on a massive scale, and in an affordable manner, to help people make an internal change.

Identifying and understanding the true causes and effects of a problem is the beginning of effective problem-solving. We cannot abandon our attempts to deal with the effects of the ghetto problem—the drug-treatment centers, the homeless shelters—but we must also turn our attention to the causes of the ghetto problem—the very minds of the people who live there. That is where the Ghetto Solution lies. Simba is one such solution.

Many people want to build institutional monuments. Simba builds human monuments. It changes lives and seeks to create multi-generational legacies of love, acceptance, patience, kindness, success, health, and wealth.

What God truly intended for his people.

—R.J. Gilbert

Roland's
Acknowledgments

"Life has meaning only in the struggle. Triumph or defeat is in the hands of the Gods... So let us celebrate the struggle!"

—Swahili Warrior Song

I want to thank all of the organizations and nameless individuals who are in the struggle with me to save our children, our future, and our country from self-destruction. I particularly want to thank the PSI World Corporation of San Rafael, California, (their quest is for world peace) for the "I AM" concept and many other concepts that have enriched my life. And a special thanks to Osa Russell who got me started on my journey of personal growth.

Michael Holland, Vernal Martin, Joshua B. Nichols, Charles Ransom, Rashid A. Shahid and Donald Walker your vision, love, faith, hard work and courage created Simba. Thank you. I love you.

I want to thank my wife Alyce, the most courageous person I know and who stands with me against all odds.

My Simba brothers and sisters, thank you for teaching me the true meaning of love and family.

Jawanza Kunjufu, thank you for having the courage to speak the truth with love and for planting the Simba seed in my heart.

Thank you our Simba children, seeing you grow beyond your limitations has been my continuing motivation—and especially you, Robert Johnson, for choosing to be the kind of man that inspires me, I love you.

Thanks to my publisher, Wayman Spence, for your friendship and faith in me and my vision. I am also grateful to Mark Patz for his insightful editing of the manuscript.

Robert Allen and Jess Mowry, your advice was invaluable, thank you.

Thank you God for the vision and the provision and especially for Christopher Billups and Keith Ragsdale, two young giants in the struggle.

Cheo's
Acknowledgments

Much praise and thanks to the creator for bringing me and mine to this point in time. To the ancestors for their struggle and victory passed down through the generations: Turner, Garvey, Vessey, Martin, Malcolm, and Newton; Tubman, Wells, Walker, and Hansberry; Wright, Dubois, and Baldwin. The spirit of these brothers and sisters let me know I wasn't the first, nor will I be the last, African in America to continue the struggle.

Everyone in Simba had a hand in this some way or another. There are too many names to list here. However, I would like to personally thank: my co-writer, Roland Gilbert, whose positive influence has changed my life; Jess Mowry, a real friend; Robert L. Allen and *The Black Scholar* magazine, whose insight and feedback during the early stages helped tremendously; Marie Dutton Brown; Dr. Jawanza Kunjufu; Dr. Nathan Hare; Blanche Richardson of Marcus Books; Dr. Wayman Spence; my extended Simba family and my family; African writers everywhere committed to recording and creating stories that celebrate our greatness; and most of all, my wife, Raina, whose unending love, constant support, and creative input helped me finish the book.

Introduction

A Father's Legacy

On a wet, rainy night in 1984, a father tucked his son into bed, opened a can of beer, and stared patiently out the back window of an old, beat-up blue van that he and his son called home. The musty smell of soggy clothes, sweat, and sex soaked the van's interior. Blankets, dirty clothes, beer cans, and cigarette butts are scattered everywhere.

Outside, raindrops trickled down the van's fogged-up windows and the glow from the tail lights of a passing car flooded the city street with red neon. The hiss of tires rolling across wet pavement muffled the footsteps of a man now just outside the van.

"Polecat, you in there?" the man muttered.

Polecat—or Boots, depending on how you knew him—rubbed his hand over the mist-covered back window, recognized his buddy, and opened the van's back door. The two friends crawled up to the front of the van and sat down. Looking at the marks on his hands and arms, Boots found just the right spot to shoot another world into his left arm. As the heroin flooded his mind and body, the needle fell from his grasp and his head began its familiar nod—first forward, then straight back, where it remained, slowly bobbing like a buoy at low tide. His friend picked up the needle and began the same ritual.

Parked on the corner of Eighth and Union Streets, the van sat in the heart of the Acorn housing projects in West Oakland. These squat and shabby duplexes, with walls patch-painted in decaying shades of yellow, brown, and red, looked more like crumbling military barracks from another era than civilian housing. Their bar-covered windows and fragile-looking doors stirred a sense of danger and vulnerability.

Clotheslines sagging with sheets, pants, shirts, and underwear hung motionless in the backyards. A few blocks up the street, a row of once refined Victorian houses stood, slowly falling apart. Some, burned out, had black, soot-covered awnings, crumbling porches, caved-in roofs, and boarded-up windows. Others were overrun with weeds, iron pipes, broken glass, and garbage. Still, this row of old abandoned homes was the most popular "playground" in the neighborhood. Every day while children played amid the decay, anxious drug dealers lingered and watched.

As morning sunlight streamed through the van's windshield, Polecat got up, grabbed a blanket, and staggered to the back, where his three-year old son lay curled up on a pillow. He placed the blanket over the sleeping child, hesitated briefly, then turned and crawled back to the front of the van.

Another day had begun in West Oakland. Another day for Milford (a.k.a. Boots or Polecat) and his son Milford, Jr. (a.k.a. Squirt) to find some place to live, something to eat, and someone to love.

The cold realities of ghetto life came early for Squirt. Abandoned by his crack-addicted mother at three days of age, Squirt was left under the custody of his father, who also abused drugs. By the time he was three years old, Squirt had already adopted a particular set of values and formed his own unique personality. Behavioral "programs," like thievery, irresponsibility, and apathy had been passed on to Squirt—both consciously and subconsciously—by his father. Four years later, when his father died from drug-related AIDS complications, Squirt inherited a legacy of bitterness, ignorance, and anger.

What becomes of a child growing up under such dire conditions, and what are his chances of becoming a productive adult? Are the "sins of the father" destined to be played out by the son all over again? The answers lie in understanding what "sins" are passed on and why they exist in the first place.

Born on July 21, 1943, Squirt's father came from a family of seven girls and three boys. He grew up in the projects of West Oakland when things were relatively calm (as compared to the drive-by violence and drug-related crime that preys on the community today). The area was highly industrial, with many factories and ship-wrecking yards. The projects—built shortly after World War II—quickly attracted unskilled laborers, discharged military personnel, and unemployed shipwreckers. Most of these people were part of a large contingent of African Americans who had migrated from Louisiana and Texas because of the availability of wartime jobs at the Port of Oakland and the Oakland Army Base.

In 1950, when Milford was only seven, his mother and father separated. Mary Gates Lewis, his mother, was left with ten children to raise on her own. Like so many African-American boys, Milford grew up without the constant presence of a black man in his life.

Always wanting but never having is a perpetual state for many ghetto children. Milford was no different. He saw all the affluence and material prosperity that society had to offer, but lacked the means of getting his fair share. Like many of the looters during the Los Angeles Rebellion of 1992, Milford believed everything he stole was owed to him—that because of his dire circumstances, he was justified in taking anything he wanted from a society where the "haves" and the "have-nots" are supposed to be equal.

From early childhood, Milford had a habit of "finding" things and putting them in his pocket. When he was nine he broke into a fish tackle store and stole some reels. He gave some away and buried the rest in the backyard. At fourteen, he and his friends went down to the train station yard, broke into a boxcar, and stole some bicycles. He gave those away too—everyone who wanted a bicycle got one. However, when his mother saw her front yard cluttered with bicycles, she called the police.

Milford went to Juvenile.

Milford's knack for theft and ability to open locks earned him the nickname, "Polecat." He was slick and sought after by people in the neighborhood whenever they were locked out of their house or car. They'd knock on the door of the Lewis house and ask Polecat to help them get in.

Although he never had much to give, Milford was generous, sharing whatever he stole. He'd often go to Fruit Town and get vegetables and produce to take home to his mother. When he brought expensive things home, he'd say he just "found" them, even if their price tags were still stuck on them.

There was something extraordinary about Milford Lewis; his good nature and warm heart put you at ease, he could take your wallet from your pocket while smiling at you. He was a smooth criminal.

Seemingly trapped, and often without much hope for making it the "right" way, Milford dropped out of school in the ninth grade. He never took a job to speak of and yet always found a way to hustle money. One day, he set a car on fire for five dollars—just took a can of lighter fluid and poured it all on the top of a convertible and threw a match on it. Milford had already mastered the first law of ghetto survival: "do whatever it takes to get over."

Milford also had his share of close encounters with the law. One day, about six police officers came to his house looking for him. He shouted to his sister, "Don't open the door until I say!" as he ran upstairs and escaped by jumping out of a second-story window onto a roof of another building, then climbing down the side.

Running from the police soon became second nature to Milford. His life revolved around getting enough money to support his drug habit, and that usually meant stealing whenever he got a chance. When the Acorn housing projects were first built, Milford and a friend broke into an apartment hoping to rob someone they thought wasn't home. But he was. As Milford was going up the stairs, the man shot him in the head and the arm. Milford ran out of the apartment, and later that night the police found him, bloody and semi-conscious, under a car. When they took him to a nearby hospital, he wouldn't let anyone touch him. With bullet wounds from a .22, he lay on the gurney saying, "Don't you touch me until my mama gets here." The police called his mother, who came to the hospital and gave the doctors permission to treat him.

As an adult, Milford attracted the admiration of a young woman named Quita Bailey. Besides their mutual attraction for each other, they shared a common habit: drugs. It was heroin for Milford and crack cocaine for Quita.

After a while, it became obvious that Quita wanted more from Milford. She wanted a serious commitment and needed more love than Milford could give her. In fact, they were both very needy people, feeding off each other and supporting each other's drug habit. When they were high, the world was beautiful and their love seemed strong. So when Quita became pregnant and Squirt was born, she wanted Milford to marry her. He refused. Quita literally threw the three-day-old Squirt at him.

Her resentment towards her son festered until, when Squirt was only five months old, Quita tried to choke him, because Milford still wouldn't marry her. To Quita, Squirt had stolen the love she thought Milford once had for her. She didn't want the baby because Milford didn't want her. Eventually, she gave up on Milford and left the projects, leaving her infant son behind.

Shortly after Quita left, Milford went to live with a friend, Jennifer, who became a sort of surrogate mother to Squirt. She changed his diapers, fed him, bathed him, and bought him clothes. Milford would sometimes steal baby food, toys, and even clothes for Squirt. One day, Jennifer told Milford how he could get all the money he needed for Squirt. She took him down to the Welfare office and helped him fill out papers to get Squirt on public assistance. For the next three years, Milford and Squirt lived with Jennifer and her boyfriend in West Oakland's Kirkum Court housing projects. But as Squirt got older, he became harder to handle and eventually too much for Jennifer. Once again, Milford and his son packed their bags and hit the streets. For the next several months, they found shelter in a parked van.

Eventually they moved in with Milford's mother, but Milford's drug habit caused problems. He stole money, food, and belongings from his mother, and made a habit of bringing his friends over to shoot up drugs when she was at work. The small, one-bedroom apartment became a popular drug depot for Milford's friends. He never cleaned up after himself, and the carpet in the apartment was often burnt by the cigarettes he dropped after he passed out from the heroin he injected. The four-year-old Squirt would often sit alone in the apartment watching TV while his father lay passed out on the floor.

But Milford's drug addiction didn't stop him from *trying* to be a good parent to Squirt. He always took Squirt wherever he went and didn't expect his mother to take care of him. He bathed him, fed him, and he took him on his motorcycle wherever he went. Still, in many cases, he took Squirt places the child should never have been, allowing him to see things he never should have seen. When Squirt saw his dad steal things, he learned it was OK to steal. And since he often saw his father and his friends use drugs, he learned that drugs were just something that all adults did whenever they wanted to "relax" or "have fun."

Without much guidance and often alone, Squirt found his way around the kitchen easily. As a five-year-old, he could cook, often fixing his own breakfast. Squirt also knew where his father kept his needles—behind some jars in a kitchen cabinet. Milford, usually too high to get up, would send Squirt next door to deliver and pick up drugs. Milford never got help for his addiction. He denied his drug problem and its affect on Squirt. When his family protested, he would simply say, "I know, I know. I'm the black sheep of the family." When Milford's drug problem became too much for his mother to handle, she moved into a senior citizen's complex, and Milford and Squirt had to find a new place to live.

Squirt grew up fast. By the time he was five, his father had taught him everything the child needed to know to survive on the streets. Every time he saw someone he knew, he'd ask for a dollar. If they didn't have a dollar, he'd ask for fifty cents, or a quarter, or fifteen cents. He had watched his father get money that way. Squirt also knew how to defend himself. He told his auntie, "If anybody bothers you, stab 'em in the stomach with a knife. That'll kill 'em."

By the time Milford turned forty, he was an old man. A lifetime of drug abuse, incarceration, irresponsibility, and emotional and physical violence had aged him beyond his years. He had lived his life like a puppet on a string, oblivious to the devastating toll his actions would have on his own life. As his body weakened, he knew it would only be a matter of time before he died. And he didn't care. He knew he wouldn't be around long enough to see his son reach nine or ten, since he had developed an inflammation of the heart and refused to be operated on, preferring just to wait for his time to die.

During the last year of Milford's life, he lived with his older brother, Marvin, while Squirt lived with his auntie, Marlene. Milford's health continued to deteriorate. He went into

Highland Hospital for tests, but signed himself out before the results came in. The next day when Marvin came home, he noticed how weak and tired his brother looked and decided that he'd better take him back to the hospital. On their way, they stopped at a Quik Way hamburger stand and got some food. Milford told Marvin that he didn't want to go back to the hospital. They sat and talked about it for over two hours, until finally Marvin convinced his brother that he had to go back. Once they arrived, the nurses admitted Milford, and Marvin took a seat in the waiting room.

After two hours of waiting, Marvin was told by a nurse that Milford wouldn't be able to go home until more tests were run. So Marvin went in to see his brother, taking him some cigarettes and magazines. Milford asked his brother to stay the night with him, but Marvin, who had other obligations, left.

He did not know he would never see his brother alive again.

Before Milford died, he asked his sister, Marlene, to take care of Squirt for him. Squirt was with Marlene on the way to the hospital when his father died.

Milford was only forty-four years old.

Milford's tragic life is a paradigm of the ghetto experience for many black men. Raised in an environment of poverty and hopelessness, Milford never really made it to manhood—in the physical sense yes, but not in the intellectual or emotional sense. However, his influence on his son's life was profound. Squirt loved his father and soaked up all the experiences his father had exposed him to, including his unhealthy relationships with women. By the time Squirt was seven years old, he was getting into fights at school, messing around with girls, and stealing. It looked as if he were doomed to follow in his father's tragic footsteps.

Then, a year after his father died, Squirt was given the opportunity to defy the odds against him.

A group called Simba, Inc., visited Squirt's school. Simba's founder, Roland Gilbert, was there and he talked to Squirt and the other boys about the things they would learn in the group. He explained that Simba had trained African American men who would teach and help the boys to grow up to become responsible, caring men.

That fall, Squirt began going to Simba's bi-weekly meetings

after school. As he sat in the first meeting, Squirt couldn't wait to play board games, watch videos, or go outside and play basketball. He thought Simba would be just like the after-school recreation center down the street. But it wasn't. The Simba leaders asked Squirt questions about how he felt and what he thought. They made him feel important. Sitting in a circle with the other boys and the men, he began to learn the importance of self-control and self-expression. The leaders introduced him to concepts like peace of mind, self-honesty, and responsibility. Squirt learned relaxation techniques and ways to let go of his anger. The men taught him about the greatness of his African ancestors and helped him to see his own greatness.

Over the next few years, Squirt learned that, regardless of his circumstances, he always had the power of choice, and that only he could decide how he thought, felt, and acted. When Squirt turned twelve, he began his year-long "rites-of-passage" training, required for all Simba boys. And he was ready. He had gained confidence and pride, but more importantly, he had learned to temper it by showing concern for his Simba brothers and other people. The emotional and psychological scars of his early childhood had begun to heal, though it might still take him the rest of his life to fully understand who his father was and why his life was so tragic.

Simba helped Squirt break the deadly cycle of ignorance, pain, and early death that grips the lives of the people in the ghetto. It changed his life.

Roland Gilbert believes that African American men are destroyed when they are boys, not when they reach adulthood. So he set up Simba, Inc., to intervene in boys' lives, to change their perspectives and expectations, to give them hope and the knowledge that choice, persistent action, faith, and God—not circumstance—determine the course of one's life.

A Man Takes Responsibility
For The Way
He Thinks, Feels, And Acts

"No systematic effort toward change has been possible, for, taught the same economics, history, philosophy, literature and religion which have established the present code of morals, the Negro's mind has been brought under the control of his oppressor. The problem of holding the Negro down, therefore, is easily solved. When you control a man's thinking you do not have to worry about his actions. You do not have to tell him not to stand here or go yonder. He will find his 'proper place' and will stay in it. You do not need to send him to the back door. He will go without being told. In fact, if there is no back door, he will cut one for his special benefit. His education makes it necessary."

Dr. Carter G. Woodson
January, 1933
The Mis-Education Of The Negro

Chapter 1

Growing Pains

My mom was reared in a little town called Glencoe, Louisiana. She is a strikingly beautiful woman of mixed ancestry. Her father was a Frenchman, her mother French and African American. In the sixth grade, she was forced to leave her segregated school to work full-time in the sugar cane fields of Louisiana. She never returned to school.

As an adult, she did day work in the homes of well-to-do white professionals in Los Angeles, as well as taking meticulous care of her own house and children. She would get up before dawn and take the long bus ride to the other side of town to earn money to buy the little extras for her family.

My dad was born in Milton, Louisiana, and raised in Beaumont, Texas. He stood over six feet tall and had coal-black skin and wavy, black hair. He was a dynamic, handsome man, who had to fight off the ladies, both white and black. His beauty and brawn were his "gifts" and he used them to build a life for our family. They were all he had. His education had stopped at the third grade, and he couldn't read or write.

When I was about thirteen years old, my friends and I would make money by robbing people at night. I would just walk down the street and whoever approached us would be a potential mark. I did most of the "work" and my friends were my backup. I'd walk up to a person and pull out my switchblade knife while my friends surrounded him. It worked every time.

Eventually, a friend and I upgraded this robbery routine to taxi cabs. We would hail a passing cab, or call one. When it arrived we'd hop in the back seat and quickly call out a destination. When the driver turned around to start the car, I would put my switchblade to his throat, and my buddy would take his money. One night we did this on Central Avenue, a main street in South Central Los Angeles. Everything went as planned. The driver stopped, we got in, I pulled my blade and held it to his throat. But he wouldn't give me his money. He started blowing the horn and screaming for help. So I stabbed him in the neck.

But he wouldn't shut up. He kept screaming!

I stabbed him repeatedly, screaming, "Die, Motherfucker! DIE!"

He wouldn't.

The next thing I knew, the police were pulling us out of the car.

They took us to the Newton Street police station. We made up a story about the cab driver trying to rob us, but the police didn't buy it. They eventually released my friend to his parents, but they kept me and sent me to Juvenile Hall until my trial.

While I awaited trial, my mom and dad came to see me. I told them the same lie I had told the police. My mom believed me but my father knew better. I was my mom's baby. She was always there for me right or wrong. I didn't really appreciate it at the time, I just thought that was what she was supposed to do.

(Looking back, I wish she could have been there for me without believing my lies and buying my bullshit when she knew I was wrong. Her acceptance of them only helped me continue to believe that I was smarter and better than other people and that I could get away with anything. For much of my life, I acted out this "program" [habitual thinking pattern] in broken relationships, drug abuse, crime, and self-gratification at the expense of others.)

At Juvenile Hall, Dad had let Mom do the talking. When my trial came up, I received two years' probation and was released into the custody of my parents. Later, when we got home, Dad tried to talk to me, but his anger led him to curse and scream. When that didn't work, he pleaded and tried to reason with me. I didn't even hear a word he said. I was so used to my mother protecting me from him that I didn't think that my father really counted. Unfortunately, Dad didn't know how to relate to a male child. He never hugged me, never showed me how to express my feelings, and never showed me that it was OK for a man to make mistakes and be vulnerable.

For all his shortcomings, my father was a hard-working man and a good provider. But although we lived together, he spent almost no time with me. He was physically there, but absent in relationship to me. All I knew of him was from observation. What I learned from him about being a man was that it was important to be strong, to never tell anybody about my business, and to take shit from nobody. We never really talked about life and being a man. Somehow it was assumed this would happen automatically. It didn't.

My teenage rites-of-passage into relationships with women was mentored by my peers. The blind leading the blind. All we knew about women we learned from the ghetto community, television, and movies. I cannot remember, ever, in school, at home, in church, or anywhere else being taught how to have a relationship with a woman as a human being who is a complete person.

I met Janet when I was thirteen. We thought we were in love and almost immediately began having sex regularly. Janet lived with her grandmother, but her grandmother had no idea we were having sex. It was always so easy for us to sneak and be together. Janet was a nice girl who trusted me and believed what I told her. She had no idea that I didn't know what I was doing, although I'd been having sex since I was eight, I still didn't know which way was up. Janet got pregnant a few months after we met. When she told me she was pregnant she apologized for getting "us" into trouble. I immediately disappeared. I thought she was just trying to trap me into marrying her and that's why "she" got pregnant. All of my friends agreed.

Eventually, Janet and her grandmother showed up at my house. My mom and Janet's grandmother talked. They worked everything out and I stopped seeing Janet. Weeks later I had heard something about her getting an abortion. I never gave it a second thought.

My first exposure to adult nightlife also came early. When I was sixteen, my cousin Harold and I frequented a nightclub on Broadway near Slauson, in South Central Los Angeles. The Broadway Club was South Central's very own "Sugar Shack." On a typical Saturday night, black folks from all around L.A. came to socialize, dance, and see some of the best local entertainers perform. The main attractions were the comedy and dance shows that played there regularly. Slappy White and others of his genre would perform there nightly. When live bands weren't performing, the DJ played music by people like Aretha Franklin, Marvin Gaye, and Little Stevie Wonder. All kinds of people partied at The Broadway—everyone from young "girl-next-door" types to college coeds to seasoned "working girls." They all found their way through the club's doors. Pimps, dope pushers, players, hustlers, working stiffs, military men, and wanna-be movie stars came for the beautiful women, good food, and high times that were guaranteed at The Broadway.

About three years earlier, the club had been converted from an old, closed-down movie theater. With its silver and black art deco-styled architecture, neon lights, and a huge, lit-up marquee above, the club was hard to miss. Brothers coasted by the club in long Lincoln Continentals, Cadillacs, and Chevrolets, to check out the women standing in line. A big searchlight in the parking lot across the street cut through the blackness, beckoning us to come and turn a typical Saturday night into an event to remember.

The first night Harold and I went, I had practiced "the game" I was supposed to run on the doorman in case he questioned my age. Harold was over twenty-one, but I was still only sixteen, although I was big for my age and looked very mature. Before we left for the club, Harold coached me on how to act. "Just look mean, man. Don't smile, and when you get to the door, just say something cool to the doorman... you'll get in," he said.

When we arrived, it was very crowded. A long line of people snaked around the corner, to the next block.

When we finally got to the door, Harold recognized the brother collecting the cover charge. He started to converse with him, to run interference for me.

"Hey cat, what's happening? You talk to Marvin since he been out the joint?" said Harold.

"Naw, man, I ain't seen nor heard from the cat," said the doorman.

"This here is my cousin, Roland. Just moved here from Detroit," said Harold.

The doorman looked me up and down very suspiciously.

"You twenty-one man?"

I reached into the inside pocket of my suit jacket, took out a roll of dollar bills and handed him two. Then casually I said: "No, I'm not... I'm twenty-four, man."

"Yeah?" asked the doorman.

"Yeah, last time I checked," I said.

I breathed a sigh of relief as we moved past the doorman and a light-skinned sister stamped my hand.

The club was crowded. The sound of loud music, laughter, and conversation greeted us as we entered the restaurant part of the club. Next to music, The Broadway's restaurant was probably its second biggest attraction. You could get red beans and rice, fried chicken, catfish, black-eyed peas, corn bread, collard greens, smothered pork chops, BBQ ribs, and simply the best sweet potato pie in all of South Central. The restaurant alone probably took in more money for take-out orders in one night than they made at the door in a week.

The dance floor and bar were upstairs. We walked up and found two empty chairs at a small cocktail table by the bandstand. It was dark, but the glow from the red candles on the tables gave the room plenty of light to operate. We sat down and immediately went to work.

"Damn, she's built like a brick house!" Harold whispered.

"You see that one over there? No, over there... look at the table across from us," I said. Pointing to a sister sitting at a table with her friends, I told Harold that she was the one I was going to leave the club with. I couldn't take my eyes off her. I know she saw me staring, but I didn't care. I was in love. The candle-light shimmered against her face and when she looked up and smiled at me, it was all over.

I got up and headed over to her table, but before I got there, three brothers came by and whisked all of her party up onto the dance floor. I watched her dance. She was about six feet tall with the longest, most beautiful legs I had ever seen. When I saw her full hips and beautiful smile, I knew I wanted her for myself.

Her name was Velma Jean Jeter. She was a junior at Fremont High School. She and her girlfriends came to the club every week and the doorman always let them in. She said he knew they were under twenty-one, but he liked one of her girlfriends and he always flirted with the rest.

"We just bat our eyes and act like we like him and he lets us in every time," she said.

"I wished that worked for me," I said.

We sat at my table all night and talked about everything. By the time the club began to close, we were already talking about whether or not I could go with her to her school prom.

After that night at the club, we began to see each other every day of the week. We were both "sprung" like spring chickens in love. She was a very quiet, homebody kind of girl. I was always the dominant one in the relationship. And even though we were the same age, she looked up to me.

After our second date, we began to have sex regularly. When she became pregnant with my son a year later, there was no doubt in my mind that I was the father. I knew I wanted my son and her, and that we all would be together. But somehow it just made "natural" sense to me to convince Velma, just before our son was born, to say the baby belonged to someone else. Someone who could afford to pay for the child and support it. I made her say it was one of the guys who had been at her table the night I met her. She reluctantly went along with my scheme and put his name down as the father on my son's birth certificate.

Well, it turned out the guy I picked was paralyzed from the waist down and could not father a child. At the time, no one could have told me that you shouldn't do things like that to people you love. In the ghetto culture, loving someone never comes before "getting over,"—and "getting over," by any means necessary, is everything. It defines you as a man. Accepting responsibility is weak, and for squares.

I loved Velma like I have never loved anyone else. She was my first love. After high school, we got married. By the time I was nineteen, we had another son. She was very caring and nurturing and we really enjoyed the outdoors. We would go on picnics or to the beach with our children. I loved my sons and I'd take them with me everywhere. It was important to me to try and be a good father to them. All Velma ever wanted to do was love me, but my ghetto programming left me incapable of accepting or returning that love.

By age ten, all I "knew" about women and relationships was that men beat up women, that men had to keep women in line, and that women were emotional and stupid, made to be conquered. Furthermore, I had learned that a man must never be weak for a women, that it was acceptable to lie to a woman to get sex, that a woman will get pregnant to trap you (mama's baby, daddy's maybe), and many other "jewels" of misconception that are far too numerous to mention.

It was a real challenge being young, stupid, and programmed in the ghetto.

I met a man named Rick Bales in the early spring of 1966. He operated the huge Rockport milling machine at North American Rockwell where we both worked. He used the machine to cut large blocks of steel down to sizable parts which the rest of us could then use to make more detailed parts, some of which were for the first shuttle in the Apollo Space Program. I was nineteen, and had been trained as a milling-machine operator by one of those poverty programs set up in the ghetto to help folks get job skills.

As a new trainee, I was amazed at the size of the machine and at the speed at which Rick could cut steel. The sound of the rotating teeth biting into the solid block of steel was deafening. With even a slight error in judgment or control, the operator could easily be maimed or killed. I worked with a much smaller milling machine, the Bridgeport. As I cut through a spaceship control panel with the machine's razor-like teeth, I realized my carbide-tip tool was missing. I approached Rick and asked to borrow his. He smiled. The Rockport unnerved me, and Rick picked up on this. He assured me that he knew what he was doing and experience had taught him the limits of his machine. With a wry smile he said, "...and if I'm wrong—fuck it!"

I wondered just who this little white man with such a casual concern for his life was. Rick, about 5'6", with sandy blond hair, reminded me of the Pillsbury Doughboy. He was in his mid-twenties and had a jovial personality and a devil-may-care attitude about life. We became great friends.

We had well-paid jobs, security, healthcare, pensions, paid vacations, and more. Rick was a confirmed bachelor. I had a wife, two children, a brand new 1966 blue Mustang convertible, and I was renting a nice home in a good neighborhood. I was a boy from South Central Los Angeles who barely graduated high school with a "D" average. And yet, I was now living the so-called American Dream.

But my ghetto mentality would not support this new

lifestyle. My ghetto belief system told me that working a job like that was for "squares." The workers at Rockwell were mostly old, white men—with a couple of black men here and there. And they were there for life!... If I didn't know anything else, I knew I didn't want to cut steel for the rest of *my* life. I wanted to "get over."

What mattered most to me was fast cars, faster women, money, control, and excitement. My "ghetto reality" said that these things were more important than my family and other people. It said that everyone would love and respect me if I had these things, if I lived that way.

I didn't know I had a choice.

I began talking to Rick about my dissatisfaction with the job and how I wanted more. I don't remember which one of us first thought of robbing a bank, but early one morning as we were closing up—we worked the swing shift at the plant— we began to discuss robbery. I guess a bank just came naturally to us. At first it was more of a challenge, we were just curious to see if we could figure out how to do it without getting caught; I don't think we really believed we would actually do it.

We decided to pick a bank with easy freeway access because we reasoned that the highest risk of capture would be during the getaway. So we got a AAA freeway map and started to locate our target. We chose the city of Santa Monica because the freeway system gave quick access to the 405 freeway to Sacramento or San Diego, and Interstate 10 to all points east. We took the yellow pages and the map and began to mark the banks on streets near freeway exits. After this we spent a couple of weeks driving the freeway exits to the banks, marking and timing the routes.

We selected a Bank of America nestled in a residential community. The front of the bank was on a major thoroughfare, but the rear door and parking lot led to tree-lined streets in a quiet neighborhood. These near traffic-less streets lead to a freeway on-ramp.

Perfect.

Next, we inspected the bank interior and personnel, casing the joint thoroughly. Since the bank was in a white neighborhood, Rick did the interior inspections and drew a detailed, color diagram. There were no visible cameras and no guard.

Perfect.

On Fridays, six to eight tellers worked cashing a lot of payroll checks. We decided to hit the bank on a Friday before 2 p.m. in order to get the most money and not get caught in a traffic jam during our getaway.

At some point during all this, this curiosity/ghetto mentality-born fantasy of robbing a bank, somehow became a reality. Rick got two .38 caliber revolvers. We had meeting after meeting discussing alternative ways of going into the bank, robbing it, and escaping. Should we walk in from the main street and run out the back to a parked car, or should we drive up to the back door and leave the engine running? What clothes should we wear? What should we carry the money in? Should we rent a car, steal a car, or use our own? Should we disguise ourselves, and if so, how? Do we drive the getaway car in the same clothes we robbed the bank in?

Once we answered these questions, we would be ready.

The day of the robbery was a beautiful, sunny, spring day. The blue jays were singing in the trees in my backyard and there was a light, cool breeze in the air. Standing in my underwear, I closed the back door, walked back to my bedroom and began getting dressed. The kids were spending a few days with our folks and the house was unusually quiet. The only sounds were of morning, and my wife in the bathroom preparing herself for the day.

There was a knock at the door.

I opened it, and there stood Rick in his blue full-body coveralls zipped in the front from his crotch to his neck. His scraggly, brownish beard covered the collar where the zipper stopped high, underneath his chin. He looked good with dyed-brown hair. He reminded me of a plumber or any other number of laborers. But the shiny new businessman's briefcase he was carrying was totally out of place.

I put on a two-piece business suit, a crisp, white shirt, and a tie. After making sure my clothes were in order, I stepped into my blue, full-body coveralls, and zipped up. I checked my briefcase once more for the receipt book, brushes, and other household items I filled it with. I put my gun in the pocket of my coveralls and stood looking at myself in the bedroom mirror. With my light, tanned skin, processed hair, and my thick, black mustache curving down the sides of my mouth to my chin, I looked Mexican or Indian or maybe middle-eastern— but certainly not African. (Of course I was trying to be white but didn't know it).

On the way to the bank, I was silent and calm in my blue Mustang with the top up. A lady friend of mine was behind the wheel and Rick was in the back seat. We had practiced the approach and getaway many times and now we were really going through with it. Everyone knew what to do.

She pulled into the rear parking lot. Rick and I got out empty handed and walked into the bank. The bank was quiet and calm, with maybe ten or fifteen customers split between four teller stations. Without hesitation, I pulled out my gun and yelled, "This is a holdup!"

Rick had his weapon out and a cloth bag to hold the money. He went to the first line. *Nobody* moved. I mean, nobody moved! They didn't give Rick any money or say anything. Everybody in the bank was just standing there looking at us for about a ten-second eternity.

Then I grabbed an elderly white woman by the hand, pointed my gun at her head, and said, "Everybody down on the floor. Give us all the money or she dies!"

The tellers immediately began putting all the money in the bag. We hit all of the tellers' windows, got the money, and ran out of there in about sixty seconds, total.

I jumped into the back seat of our car while Rick got into the front. My lady friend pulled out of the lot, turned right into the residential neighborhood behind the bank, and headed towards the freeway traveling at a moderate speed, as planned. While she was driving, Rick quickly dumped the cash into her big shoulder bag. We unzipped our coveralls and revealed our suits and ties. Then we parked two blocks away from the bank and parallel to the main thoroughfare, stuffing our coveralls into the shoulder bag.

Rick got out, pulled off the stolen license plates we had fastened over the real ones with rubber bands, put the plates in his briefcase, and leisurely walked towards the main street to wait for the bus. My friend continued to drive the car towards the freeway on-ramp. After a few blocks, we stopped again and I got out. Immediately, I began going door-to-door, selling my household items. I saw police cars patrolling the neighborhood, but they never stopped me as I sold my wares and made my way to the next bus stop.

We got away with about $16,000, although the news reports said $30,000. After that, I hooked up with some of my old buddies who had been in gangs with me, and we started planning robberies. Eventually, we had a gang of our own, and started hitting a lot of banks. Although I never went into any more banks, we planned the robberies, provided the money and weaponry required. We had turned bank robbery into a fine science—or so we thought.

It took the FBI about a year to catch us.

One day they came to my door with a search warrant. They looked everywhere, but found nothing. They didn't arrest me, but a month later someone called me and asked me to come down to the Santa Monica police station. They said it had something to do with my car being a stolen vehicle. When I got there, I went in a room and started talking to a cop about my car, where, without my knowing, they had the old woman I had held a gun to in the next room, looking at me through a two-way mirror.

After about five minutes the cop got up and walked out. Within a minute, he came back and put me under arrest. Then there was a line-up and I was picked out from the rest. They tried to convict me of all of the robberies, but they couldn't prove my involvement. But they did prove that first robbery.

The judge gave me twenty-five years, with no parole for at least eight years and four months. But God had another plan. My mother hired an attorney who discovered that my partner had only been sentenced to ten years for the same crime by the same judge. We went back to court to protest the sentence. Our plea was denied. After several court battles, we were finally able to get a favorable decision.

My sentence was reduced to fifteen years with an "A" number, which meant that I was eligible for parole at any time. I served a total of three and a half years in the Lompoc Federal Correctional Penitentiary in northern California.

Chapter 2

Second Chance

During my time in prison, I concentrated on what I'd do when I got out. I painfully missed my wife and two sons. Whenever they would visit, watching them go was almost unbearable. I also missed the money and the carefree lifestyle I'd come to know during my bank-robbing days. All I could think about was getting out and making more money— although I had made up my mind to do it legally.

The furthest thing from my mind was getting out and enrolling in college. After all, I'd barely gotten out of high-school.

But by the day I met Bob Newcomb in the penitentiary, I was willing to listen to anything to get out of prison early. He was a math professor at the University of California, Irvine. He had the idea that there were good people in prison, that all we needed were the benefits of a good education. He talked with me and told me that I'd do well in college. He encouraged me to pursue mathematics.

I was released from prison in the fall of 1971 and immediately went to see Bob about enrolling at the university. After taking several tests and filling out applications, financial aid forms, and an assortment of other paperwork, I was admitted.

Situated amid lush, green rolling hills in a totally new community in Southern California, Irvine was a beautiful campus. The city was a Mecca for money, high technology, and the nouveau riche. We didn't have a football team, but we had a yachting club and we'd go "yachting" at Newport Beach. Even though most of the students were rich and white, I got along with everybody. We were all into experiencing new ideas and attitudes that were still in the air from the Sixties.

Bob helped me get into student housing, and my wife and

kids moved up from L.A. to live with me. At twenty-four, I was older than most of my classmates, and in many ways I felt superior to them, having had the benefits of street knowledge. But I also felt inferior as most of the kids who went to Irvine came from very well-to-do families.

My first semester, I enrolled in general education classes, many of which were sub-college level courses supposed to prime me for my freshman classes. Since Bob thought I'd do well in math, I took a pre-Algebra class. I actually liked it and earned a "B" in the class.

I began to gain confidence and slowly I worked my way through the other disciplines: Algebra, Geometry, and Trigonometry. When I finally took Calculus, I failed miserably. I hated the class. My instructor was a short, Asian man who wore a black two-piece suit with the pants' legs high above his ankle. He wore white socks, black shoes, white shirt, and a little black tie—every day.

The classroom was a big lecture hall with about 100 seats arranged in several descending tiers. He'd come in the class and say, "Good afternoon. Today we are going to discuss..." and he'd turn around and begin talking to the blackboard, working on a math problem from one end of it to the other.

I didn't know what the hell was going on.

I took the first midterm and got a "D-."

I went to talk to Bob.

"Drop the class," he said. "Take Calculus from this other guy next semester," he insisted.

So, reluctantly, I went back next semester and did as Bob suggested. This instructor was totally different. He was a tall, lanky white man, with hair down to his shoulders, and he wore blue jeans with holes in the knees. He'd walk in the room and say, "Look people, this stuff is really easy once you understand how it all works together." Then he would begin to talk to us and show us pictures. That's when I began to understand the importance of pictures. The numbers always represent a picture of something.

To help cover some of my tuition, I received financial aid, which included a grant, some loans, and work-study. My work-study job was at the university biology lab, off-campus. I did a lot of routine research and library work, as well as lab help and bottle-cleaning.

There were people there working on a cure for emphysema. They experimented with tarantulas and other creatures to study the effects of serious diseases, like cancer. One day, when I arrived at work, all of the professors and staff were talking about the big breakthrough that had happened that day. Dr. Heinz, the head of the department, had made a discovery on the emphysema project. Everyone in the building was talking about how great it was and what it meant for the department and the school.

Sometimes I worked in Dr. Heinz's office and I had always wondered why everyone was so in awe of him. He was a very tall man and he walked with a slight limp. He always wore white, starched short-sleeve shirts with a pen-holder in the breast pocket. He was from Germany and talked with a very thick accent. The day he made the breakthrough, I approached him in the library to congratulate him.

"Congratulations! You're a genius," I said.

He was very proud. He looked at me and smiled. Then, quite matter-of-factly, he said, "Roland, genius is the ability to observe the obvious." He shook my hand, smiled, then turned and walked away.

Since my release from prison, my relationship with Velma had gotten steadily worse. Even though she and the boys were living with me in student housing, I didn't spend enough time with them. I was always taking classes, working, and discovering who I was. The college experience was exciting and new and it began to totally restructure my whole life. I saw how bored Velma was at home so I got her enrolled in the university and she began taking classes.

That's when I began to notice a change. Her vision expanded. Soon a lot of things I'd been doing all along weren't acceptable anymore. She began to speak up for herself, to take positions on issues. And the "real" issue was me and other women. We started arguing about anything and everything. Her relationship with me shifted from one of *being* with me to one of *dealing* with me. After months of fighting, one day we just looked at each other, and very calmly she said, "We can't be together anymore."

"I know."

She went back to Los Angeles to stay with her mother and finish school. The kids stayed with me.

I would take my sons to stay with her and her mother every other weekend. One weekend when I arrived to pick them up, Velma wouldn't let me have them.

I was standing outside the house knocking on the door. She was standing with the boys, looking at me out of the living room window. "What are you doing? I came to get the kids," I said.

"No, you're not taking them!" she shouted.

"What are you talking about?" I yelled.

"I'm going to keep them—they're my kids!" she said.

"Open this goddamned door!" I said.

"Fuck you!" she screamed.

I got mad. I stood out there on that porch screaming and hollering for about thirty minutes. And the kids were just watching. She knew I loved my sons and she was trying to hurt me.

Eventually, I just left. I didn't want the kids to be exposed to that any longer. A few weeks later, when I came back, she let them go with me. She had realized she couldn't deny her own children a visit with their father.

Over the next year, I filed for divorce and we began to negotiate a settlement. We had been married nine years, and although we shared many loving, beautiful memories, I still didn't know how to have a real relationship with a woman.

By my third year at UC Irvine, I had developed quite well as a student. I met a beautiful young Japanese/African American girl named Juanita. She was three years younger than me and she fed into my "dominant parent" orientation. We started dating and were living together within a month. We were definitely in love and wanted to be with each other night and day.

It was her senior year and she had made plans to go to graduate school. But when she got accepted to Harvard she had mixed feelings. She told me that she didn't want to leave me. I wanted her to go. I told her it was a great opportunity and I didn't want her to sacrifice it for me. But she said it really wasn't what she wanted anymore. She wanted to stay with me and get married. I loved her, she loved me, that's all we thought we needed.

After about six months, we got married.

Juanita became a great help to me. She would take the boys

to school and help them with their homework. She was very supportive, but she also was very dependent. She needed me more than I thought I needed her. I was running around, trying to work deals, go to school, and raise my sons. She wanted me to settle down and be a husband. I didn't know how. I was always too busy and I didn't spend enough time with her.

It was our two-month "anniversary." We made big plans to go out to dinner and I was supposed to meet her at six o'clock. I was out visiting an old partner of mine and we were trying to work some new scam to make some money. When I got to the restaurant, Juanita was nowhere to be found. I looked at my watch. It was 7:30 p.m. I didn't really think anything of it at the time and I just got in my car and went home.

When I got back home she was in the shower. I went in the bathroom.

"Hi, Juanita! Why did you leave the restaurant?"

She didn't say a word.

"All right, I'm sorry I was late, but I couldn't help it." I said. "We can still go."

I opened the shower door to see her face. She was crying. I reached for her.

"Don't touch me! You don't care about me and you don't care about us! Get out! get out!"

She had realized I couldn't be what she wanted. We made up, but it still just went downhill. In two short months, it was over. I still didn't know how to have a relationship, how to be "real" with a woman.

My major difficulty throughout all my relationships was expressing honest love.

When she left me, I sent the kids to stay with Velma and I continued working and going to school. Now I had more time to devote to my studies and my aspirations. I was in my junior year and I began to think about what I wanted to do when I graduated.

I heard of a new program being offered on campus, called the "3-2 program." It enabled students in their last year of undergraduate school to simultaneously enroll in graduate courses. In effect, you could finish your undergraduate degree and then be only one year away from earning a graduate degree. I was accepted into the program and began working towards my master's degree in Administration, concentrating in operations research and finance.

By the end of the spring semester, I had applied to just about every major company in the area. They all had summer job programs and I desperately wanted "real world" experience.

About two weeks before classes were over I got a call from the telephone company. They wanted me to come in and interview. I must have impressed them, because I was hired right after my interview. During June of 1974, I started my summer assignment with Pacific Telephone and Telegraph in Anaheim, California.

I was employed as an engineer and I came in through their Summer Management Program. I had independent responsibilities just like the rest of the engineers. My assignment was to design the growth and distribution of the several telephone plants throughout Orange County. I was to modify all existing telephone lines to prepare for population growth in each city in the county. This required me to go out and look at several sites and come back and design plant cable routes and figure out the best way to route the lines.

This was quite a challenging position, particularly for someone who didn't have any engineering experience.

The office I worked in was all-white. I was the only African American person in the whole building. And at that time, I was wearing a large 'fro, platform shoes, bell-bottom pants, and wide knit ties. Everyone else in the office was very conservative. Most were in their forties. Only a couple of the other engineers would speak to me. Whatever they thought of me probably wasn't too favorable.

But their stares didn't bother me. I was too excited. This was my first real, professional position and I was determined to do the best I could. I was not even conscious of my appearance because it was normal to me. But in their environment, in their eyes, I was strange.

After I had been on the job about a week, the senior engineer, Larry Smith, called me into his office. Larry was a tall, older white man, almost totally gray. He was a compass and slide-rule kind of guy, and had one of those plastic pen holders in his shirt pocket.

Larry was always very "pleasant" to me. By "pleasant," I

mean his attitude was, "I'm going to treat everybody the same. Nobody is going to be able to say that I'm a racist." He was one of those guys who worked hard at not being a racist, without realizing that he was.

"How's the project going?" he asked.

"Very well," I said.

"I've heard that you're doing real well. As a matter of fact, you're doing so well, you're ahead of schedule. So, since you're going to have some time on your hands, I want you to take a look at this problem that we've been working on around here for some time. We haven't really been able to come up with a solution for it," he said.

He began to tell me about the Underground Construction Project. They wanted to route cable underground, but a difficulty arose whenever they wanted to run cable around corners that weren't 90-degree angles. For every non-90-degree corner in cities throughout the county, they had to have a draftsperson draw the intersection and spin the radius on a compass to find it by trial and error. The draftsperson would then read the compass and give that measurement to the engineers in the field. Then they could cut the radius into the ground and lay the cable.

Now this was time-consuming, a lot of work, and required a lot of staff. What they wanted was a formula that the engineers in the field could use. That was the problem. They had been working on it for years and hadn't found a formula that worked.

"I understand you have an excellent background in mathematics, that's why you got the job," Larry said. "So I want you to take a look at this problem and see if you can come up with something for us."

"Sure! I'd be happy to," I said.

I began discussing the problem with a few mathematicians I knew from school, but nobody had an answer. Then, after a few days, I came up with what I thought was the answer. I took it by a few professors at school and they agreed with my formula. The next morning, I rushed to work, eager to show it to my boss.

"I did it. Here's the formula," I said.

"Oh, this looks great," he said. He sat down and pushed everything off of his desk and pulled out his old compass and slide rule and began to check angles and numbers. After about ninety seconds, he put his slide rule back into his pocket, leaned back from his desk, and smiled. "Close... but no cigar. It doesn't work," he said with an air of satisfaction.

I was totally deflated.

"What?!" I said. I jumped up out of my chair and ran around next to him behind his desk to have a closer look. Then he showed it to me. He had drawn a very complex intersection and plugged the numbers into my formula, and it didn't work.

So I went back to the drawing board.

I worked on the problem every day after work. I did a computer run on it, but the computer didn't have any answers. I quickly realized that this was not a textbook problem. I'd have to find the answer in the real world. I pulled several maps of intersections and studied their respective radiuses. I went out to certain sites and measured distances and tried to check my calculations physically. I drew countless intersection configurations and tested several formulas. Several weeks went by, and I still hadn't figured it out.

Then one day, as I was sitting in my room staring at the problem on a blueprint, I saw it. The solution just popped into my head—as clear as day. I heard myself say, "That's it!" and I immediately grabbed a pencil and began diagramming the angle relationships and putting them into a mathematical formula.

The next day I went to the drafting department and had a draftsperson draw up the solution. I wrote the formula on a separate sheet of paper. Then I wrote out a qualitative "proof" of the solution on another sheet of paper. I put the final draft, the formula, and my written proof all together in a clear plastic folder to make a real presentation out of it. Then I took it into my boss.

"Here it is!" I said.

"Oh, quite impressive," he said. "OK, let's see what you got."

Once again he cleared his desk and pulled out his stuff and started working on it. "Hmm, OK, that works..." he said, talking to himself.

I could see that he was checking several configurations. This time it took him about five minutes instead of ninety seconds. Finally, he put his instruments down and leaned back.

"Well... it works," he said.

There was no smile this time. In fact, he seemed irritated.

"But you know Roland, this is quite a formidable formula," he said.

"Well, it's quite a formidable problem," I said.

He was implying that it wasn't good enough. He wanted me to make the formula simpler. The real problem, of course, was that they had worked on this problem for years without discovering *any* solution, but I had shown up and solved it in a few weeks.

The fact that I was a young, African American male made it a bitter pill for him to swallow.

The next day I saw him out in the main office area where all of the engineers worked. He was having a conversation with another engineer. All of a sudden I heard him holler out from across the room, "That was a great solution to that problem Roland! Thank you very much!"

Then he walked back to his office. When all the other engineers heard this, they came over to my desk to ask me questions and to try to figure out how my formula worked. They couldn't believe I had solved the problem, especially since they'd all tried at one time or another. After that, everybody talked to me. Now that I had done something they *couldn't*, they began to see me as an equal.

This goes back to what I had learned growing up—that I had to be twice as good as the average white boy just to make it in America. They began to use my formula in the field and it saved the company hundreds of thousands of dollars.

Was I paid anything for it? Did they give me any other recognition for it? Well, Larry's shout of thanks across the room had been it. No company bonus, no plaque or certificate. Nothing. Even during my exit interview with the personnel department, nothing was said about my formula. Finally I brought it up, only to find out that they hadn't heard anything about it! Apparently, it was the engineering department's little secret.

So, before I left, I went back to my boss and asked him to write a letter stating that I had created a formula that the company was now using which saved them money. He was reluctant, but he did it.

By the time I finished my assignment with the phone

company, I'd learned a valuable lesson about white people and power, and black people and pride.

During my last year at UC Irvine, I was recommended by the dean of the graduate school to President Carter's Presidential Management program. One thousand of the top graduate students from the very best schools across the country were recommended to this program annually. Once selected, all of the candidates convened in Los Angeles for a three-day competition of management and problem-solving skills. There were several written exams that took literally days to finish. It was a weed-out system and only 250 students would be selected. They wanted to take the cream of the crop and appoint them to work in the federal government.

The final series of tests were experimental scenarios where about eight students were put in a room and given some managerial or operational problem. My group did well and I took the leadership role, suggesting to my all-white, fellow students how we could solve the problem.

On the last day, an all-white panel of judges interviewed all of the chosen candidates. One of the questions they asked me was: "How did you feel about some of the resistance you got during the group problem-solving session?"

"If you're talking about what I felt to be racial resistance against me for taking the leadership role, I'm used to that. Oftentimes white people resent me because I'm a leader, and I'm black. I was raised right here in Los Angeles. In the ghetto. I've gone through a lot to be here," I said.

Then there was total silence. You could hear a pin drop. They just wrote notes on little notepads and stared at me.

On the third day, the results came in from all of the testing, and somehow, I'd made it.

Once I was selected to be among the 250, I was courted by several government agencies to come and work. I accepted a position with the Small Business Administration in Washington, D.C.

In that agency, I would travel all over the country as a Business Revitalization Specialist for the Neighborhood Business Revitalization program. My job was to go to various cities and work with city officials to access options for creating new business opportunities.

After I got to Washington, it quickly became apparent that

my job would require "on-the-job" training. So, after a couple weeks, my boss gave me a booklet of plane tickets, briefed me on the particular situation in each city, and sent me off. I was a rookie, but because of my presidential appointment, I was given a lot of responsibility. I had a million-dollar credit authority available to me for each city I traveled to. I represented our program's stance on issues, and I negotiated with agencies all across the country.

For someone who had robbed banks and spent time in prison, I felt very lucky to have this second chance. My new career was off to a great start and I learned some valuable lessons about the government and how things actually get done in this country. Of course, it was all politics. And that's what eventually caused things within the SBA to change drastically.

After a year or so, we had been able to leverage $200 million into a billion dollars worth of financing for new businesses across the country. Everything was going great, and then the Department of Housing and Urban Development wanted to take the administrative lead in our program. We didn't want to give it up. It came down to a lot of bureaucratic back and forth, and nothing was getting done.

Then I got a very lucrative job offer to set up a business back in California. Although I had been successful within my position at the SBA, I was sick and tired of the bureaucracy. I took that job offer, and within a few days I was back in Southern California.

I had known Chuck since kindergarten. We basically grew up together and had remained friends over the years. Now that I was living back in L.A., we began hanging out again, chasing women and working deals together.

One night he was having a get-together at his house and he wanted me to come. When I arrived, about four or five people were there. They were all sitting around drinking beer, listening to music and talking. Chuck knew that I occasionally snorted cocaine and took it upon himself to show me a new way to use it.

I sat down on the couch and had a beer, and Chuck passed me a glass pipe.

"Here, check this out," he said.

There was a bottle of 151 Rum on the table. He took a cotton ball and put it on the end of a broken coat hanger. Then he lit the rum-soaked cotton. Using it as a torch, he heated the pipe until it was hot enough to vaporize the rocks. When the vapor formed in the glass he took a hit. I took a couple of hits and not much happened. Actually, at first, I couldn't even understand why people would want to smoke it. But I did it several more times with him and soon I developed a taste for it.

Before I knew it, smoking crack became a regular part of my day.

My consulting business was going very well. In fact, I bought a house out in Huntington Beach and drove a brand new Corvette. I was living the swinging bachelor life, partying and playing that big-shot role.

One day I had an important meeting with the president of one of the companies we had invested in and I showed up "coked" out of my mind with a couple of European women I'd just met. We went in, sat down for five minutes and left. I was supposed to be there to discuss the financial strategies for the future of the company, but none of that seemed important to me anymore.

Six months from the day I'd first smoked crack, I had spent over $100,000 on it and squandered another $150,000 on business deals, a car, women, and other bullshit. I was broke and I had ruined all the business deals my partner and I had put together.

And then I just started to go straight to hell... straight down. I owed everybody money. I had even stopped paying the note on my house. I checked myself into a drug treatment program at the Care Unit at the Alta Bates Hospital in Berkeley. But it didn't work for me. I went right back to smoking crack.

I was a helpless addict and I didn't care.

I had lost everything and I had nowhere to go. I called my mother and as I knew she would, she offered to let me stay with her. She was still there for me.

One day I borrowed my sister's car. I needed to go score some coke for the weekend. Once I got it, I couldn't wait for the weekend, I started smoking right there in the car. I had owed $6,000 to a bail bondsman, had some of the money in my wallet, and the bulk of it was in the glove compartment of the car.

Somewhere along my way home, I met two women. I flashed my money to impress them and told them we could have a good time. They were into partying and so we decided to get a room at a motel. We sat up in the motel room and drank liquor and smoked, listened to music and partied.

When we ran out of crack, we went out to get some from a couple of dealers. We drove down the street and met these two guys at a vacant parking lot behind a grocery store. I got out of the car and started talking to them about what I wanted, while the girls remained in the car.

At first everything was cool. But that quickly changed when the dealers saw that I was high and loaded with cash. These guys were street dealers I had never seen before in my life. I should have been cautious or at least suspicious, but I was too high to think about that sort of stuff. I just wanted to score some more crack.

Then one of them decided he was going to rob me. We started to argue and he hit me with a two-by-four, splitting my head open. I began to scream and curse at them and fight them off. I punched one in the face and kicked the other in the groin. I was so coked up, I continued to fight without feeling anything... and I didn't go down. As we fought, the ladies took off in my sister's car, with the money still in the glove compartment. I didn't even try to stop them.

Eventually, the dealers saw that I wasn't going to go down and they just ran off. I collapsed next to some garbage dumpsters. As I lay with bruises all over my face, blood poured down the side of my head and onto my cheek. My sister's car and all of my money was gone.

Lying in a pool of my own blood, there was only one question on my mind: Where could I get some more crack?

Chapter 3

Saved

"Honey, you got to go to the hospital. You're bleeding all over the place," I heard a voice say. A lady from a nearby apartment complex had come over to help me.

"I'll be all right," I said.

"Come on and get in my car. I'm taking you to the hospital," she said. She did, and a doctor put eight stitches in my head.

Afterwards, we went back to the motel. She smoked too, so we got some more coke and started partying again. I passed out on the floor and when I woke up she was gone.

It was about 3 a.m. when I made it home. I limped to the porch of my mother's house and sat down. My head was bandaged with white, blood-stained gauze and tape. My face was scraped and bruised and my lower lip was split open. I ached from head to toe.

It all started coming back to me. I had lost my sister's car and $6,000 dollars of my own money.

It was cold out and I didn't have a jacket. But I didn't go inside. I was trying to prolong my adventure and I knew as soon as I went back in, I'd be faced with reality.

And reality scared the shit out of me.

But eventually I knew I had to go in, I had to face it.

I went in and turned on the TV. One of those late-night religious programs happened to be on, and it was as if the man on TV was talking directly to me. He said that it was never too late to change, and that God had the power of forgiveness. He said that God loved even the worst sinners, and that all I had to do was invite God into my life and allow him to save my life. I sat there in the living room in the dark and I listened to the entire program. When it was over, I fell to my knees. "God, if you just bring my sister's car back, I'll change my life," I said.

And those of you thinking at this point that the Lord has better things to do than find stolen cars for drug addicts, should take into account that the Lord's capacity for forgiveness is immeasurable, and that my prayer, though somewhat selfish, was sincere, and at that point, the only way I knew to ask for help or anything else, was to cut a deal.

So I cried and prayed, and prayed some more.

The next day we called around looking for my sister's car. It was at the police pound, and we went and got it. It was completely intact. God had answered my prayers! For the first time in my life I believed in the power of the Lord and I committed myself to changing my life.

I was saved.

The next Sunday I got baptized in church, and from that day on I clung to the Lord. It wasn't easy, but I had already been to the bottom. There was nowhere else for me to go but up.

I became an ardent student of the Bible. The Bible was my security blanket and I took it with me everywhere. I was truly "born again," and that's when I started leaving drugs alone.

I moved to Oakland in 1985. I still wanted to continue my consulting business, but I was having a hard time re-establishing myself. I couldn't get work anywhere. Eventually, I took a job at the Oakland airport as a parking booth cashier.

To some, the fact that I was now working at an airport would seem demoralizing, especially since I had accomplished so much earlier in my life—gone to college after prison and earned not one, but two degrees; been appointed by President Carter to a position with the Small Business Administration; and had been recognized nationally in *Who's Who in Finance & Industry in America.*

But somewhere along the way I had lost control of my life and now it was time to start over. But what would my mother think? What would she say about her baby making five dollars an hour as a cashier in a parking lot? I had always tried so hard to impress her. She always said, "Make your mother proud of you"—but it didn't really matter. For the first time in my life, I was OK with my situation. During many of those dark, solitary nights at the airport, I reflected on my past, and the mistakes I'd made before God had saved me.

When I first went to work at the airport, they put me in a

booth with a cashier, who showed me how to work the register, process parking slips, and run the whole booth. Initially, I worked the day shift, then they moved me to the swing shift, and finally to the graveyard shift. On a typical day I'd clock in, read the bulletin board, have some light chatter with my co-workers who were changing shifts, get out my money, check the receipts, remove the traffic cone so people could drive through, and turn on the light in my booth. At 1 a.m., the last flight would come in and it would get busy. We'd handle that flight, get everybody out, then there would be nothing until 6 o'clock in the morning.

This was my time.

There were no supervisors around and it was completely silent. With my radio tuned to a religious station, I'd just sit back and study my Bible. All those hours to just study, pray and meditate. It was wonderful!

During this time I was married to my third wife, in what was more a business arrangement than anything else. Our relationship was based on our shared passion for making money. It was purely business and I was like an "investment" for her. We were both into real estate and into finding quick ways to make money. In fact, she was more like my manager than my wife, and I was the "deal maker," scheming, planning, and executing deals. At least that was the plan.

After exactly one year, she started to lose faith.

"I've given you a year and my investment is still not paying off," she said.

She gave me two weeks to get my act together or I'd have to go. Two weeks came and went, and so did I. She petitioned for divorce, I agreed with all of the terms, and it was over.

In September of 1987, I got my own apartment. It was a three-room flat on 12th Avenue in Oakland. It was a dream for me. I had been renting out rooms or sharing my living space with others for a long time, and now I was back to having my own place.

The flat was very sunny with big windows that overlooked the backyard. The manager had just re-done the place with new paint, new linoleum, a new refrigerator—new everything. It was crisp and clean and very fresh.

A couple lived upstairs and the owner lived downstairs.

I decorated the place with inspirational poems, Bible scriptures, and "Daily Word" messages. I had a diagram called the "Walk with God," which outlined the steps all those who are born again must take. It showed the road to salvation through faith in Christ.

I would tack little index cards with spiritual or inspirational messages on the walls, on the mirror in the bathroom, the refrigerator, anywhere I happened to be. I became a hermit on 12th Avenue.

Since I worked at night I had all day to write, read and study.

In the following January, I created the design for the Ambassadors Breakfast Clubs of America. Since I had grown in Christ I'd noticed a peculiar phenomenon. There were people who were Christians in the same way they were Democrats, Republicans, doctors, managers, and so on. That is, being a Christian to them was just another part of their character.

I humbly include myself, and all Christians, to some degree, in this category, because we know the difficulty of trying to live daily for Christ in all that we do, at home, at work, and at play. Of ourselves we shall always fail, but by the word and grace of God, our savior Jesus Christ, and the Holy Spirit, we can succeed.

I committed myself to starting an organization dedicated to these part-time Christians, "moonlighting" with God. It was my first attempt to formally organize and implement a structure and system to help others choose to live more fulfilling lives. It was actually the beginning of my methodology for Simba, Inc.

My goal was to get Christians to meet daily for breakfast and use the Scriptures and mutual support to discuss and resolve day to day problems in life. Unfortunately, I could not find any Christians within my church or in outside institutions that wanted to support this idea. But the months of work I spent in designing and writing the bylaws and articles, registering the organization as a California corporation, and thinking through the entire concept, were later invaluable in designing Simba, Inc.

I participated in a march sponsored by Allen Temple for Oakland's homeless people. We marched all the way from the church at East 14th and 92nd Street down to 14th and Broadway. Along the way, I met a woman from the church, Opal. We walked and talked together. When we got downtown there was a rally at the park across the street from city hall. We listened to several speakers talk about Oakland's homeless people and the widespread poverty in the city.

Opal was a major influence on me. She was very in touch with her spirituality. She helped me see myself and the world around me in a totally different way. Opal was an insurance agent and pumped herself up with a lot of motivational tapes. Once, when we were out for a drive, she put a tape in the car stereo. It was Dennis Whaitley speaking about how Olympians train to get their goals. He said that no matter what our circumstances are, we can choose to change them. We can take a thing that looks like a huge problem and we can shift our focus about it and turn it around to create an opportunity instead of a problem. Opal talked to me a lot about personal power and how I could reach my goals.

Another person who was a great influence on me was Dr. Jawanza Kunjufu, who I first met in November 1987. As I was leaving church one Sunday afternoon, someone placed a small brochure in my hand announcing a one-day workshop on the plight of African American men and boys at St. Paul of The Shipwreck Church in San Francisco.

About twelve African American men attended. Jawanza made me aware of the national statistics showing the disastrous trends of the African American male. I highly recommend his book, *Countering the Conspiracy to Destroy Black Boys,* volumes I, II, and III, published by his company, African American Images, in Chicago, Illinois. Dr. Kunjufu emphasized the need for a one-year rites-of-passage program for African American boys.

About this time, Opal introduced me to an organization called PSI (People Synergistically Involved) World. In December, the group was hosting an educational seminar that helped people discover greater self-awareness. Opal suggested that I go. PSI is headquartered in San Rafael, California. It was founded by Thomas D. Willhite, who was trained by Alexander Everett of the now-extinct Mind Dynamics Corporation.

For most of the attendees, it was strictly a psychological seminar. But for me, it was a coming together of the spiritual and the psychological. I was already being led by the Spirit of

God, so the additional psychological awareness helped me heal some old wounds in my life that I hadn't even known I had—specifically, issues between my mother and my father.

During the workshop we went through "processing" sessions where we examined our past behavior patterns. I realized that I had always blamed my behavior on other people or circumstances. I had great excuses for why I was acting a certain way, but my behavior remained the same.

All of my growth time, from the time I was "saved" in 1984, to the time I got to the PSI World workshop in 1987, was spent in the Bible. I was discovering my spiritual power. At first I was very religious, even dogmatic. But I grew beyond religious to spiritual. And finally, psychological awareness became real for me. I realized the spiritual level is our foundation—that we are all spiritual beings living a human experience. Race doesn't matter. It's simply a diversion. It keeps us from the truth. Most of us stop at that level and don't go any deeper, to understand that it's just a superficial representation.

I tell some brothers, "I don't care if it was the Grand Dragon of the Ku Klux Klan, if he said something that I thought I could use to empower me, I'd buy it." But they don't understand that. We get caught on the material plane and don't empower ourselves because of our own prejudices. But we're all spiritual beings, we're all inter-connected. And when we really understand that, then we can understand how the Grand Dragon of the K.K.K. could have a message for us. And we can understand the Scripture that says, "God will speak to you in strange ways."

The spiritual plane controls the material plane. That's the power of faith. However, we think the other way around. We think first to manipulate material things, when the power lies in learning how to manipulate the spiritual-self. But because of our Eurocentric bias, we think in terms of counting and measuring and technology and so on. The ancient Africans, then called Kemites or Egyptians, knew the difference. This was the basis of their Mystery System.

When I had my spiritual and psychological awakening, I finally realized what it was that had happened to me. I understood that my actions came from my beliefs. My spirit had been trapped inside a belief system that said, "that's just the way I am," and "that's the way the world is." Soon I would develop the concept of Simba based on my own pain and my own awakening process. PSI World gave me the beginning of the structure of the Simba Leadership Seminar. After experiencing PSI World, I wrote my parents a letter, which I never mailed.

February 12, 1988
Dear Mom & Dad,
This is the last time you will ever hear from me until we meet in heaven. I want to tell you how I feel. I have loved you both and hated you both since I can remember. I hated you, Mom, for not touching me with real emotion. Yes, you were affectionate and responsible... you did what you were "supposed" to do but you never really touched me with your honest and true feelings. I hated Dad for not touching me with his emotions and for beating me and for not loving me and not accepting me as his son. I also hated Dad for rejecting me and telling me that I wasn't shit and that I would never be shit. I hated you both for creating a family of people who were never a people that were family. I grew up alone, never being touched inside. I have hated myself for the same reasons. You see, Mom and Dad, I treated my wives and children and friends the same way. I was affectionate but I never really let them touch me emotionally and I never really touched them emotionally. I have lived a life without trust, honesty, and real feelings. I have lived a lie. I am letting go of all this and I am forgiving me and you and Dad because you didn't mean to do it. You did the best you could, the best you knew how to do. I experienced that we are all children in adult bodies living/ acting out programs given to us by our parents or others when we were children in children's bodies. I forgive you and I love you both because I choose to change my life and touch you and my children and other people.

Your Son, Roland

Many African American males grow up as I did—with a protective mother and an absent father in a ghetto community that teaches them money is everything. Money defines who they are and what they can be. It is more important than anything, including people. They learn that circumstance and what other people do, or don't do, determines their behavior.

I created Simba, Inc., to change all this. My vision is to re-program the thinking of adults and children with the truth: People are more important than objects and each of us has the power to choose our own behavior in spite of other people and circumstances. Simba exists to save our ghetto children.

The stage was now set. All of my pain, all of my failure, all of my progress, all of my training, all of my experiences had brought me to a higher spirituality and new awakening. I was now focused on one desire: to save our ghetto children.

Chapter 4

The Birth of Simba

I loved my mornings at the airport. During those precious few moments before dawn, before the black of night diffused into a new day, I witnessed the magic and miracle of a new sunrise. The transformation never ceased to amaze me. I'd be sitting alone in my booth, usually reading or listening to a radio program, when I'd notice the night sky slowly come alive. Translucent rays would filter through dark shadows, creating a strange mixture of night and day. This was my time. When the sun finally did creep above the horizon, I envisioned myself, too, as a rising phoenix, coming out of a dark slumber.

Soon, planes would be coming in one after another, bringing a flock of people rushing to their cars. By the time I changed shifts with my co-worker, the parking lot would be filling up and I'd be anxious to leave. After work, I'd routinely get a newspaper and then head directly home. My "incubator" over on 12th Avenue was always bright and sunny and conducive to everything I wanted to do. I'd been spending most of my mornings developing my idea for Simba.

When I got home, I would begin my after-work ritual of centering myself, focusing all of my energies on positivity and inner peace. I would sit in a chair in the kitchen. With my back against the back of the chair, my feet in front of me, and my hands—palms up—on my lap, I would begin to concentrate on every inch of my body. I would close my eyes and take a few deep breaths. Slowly, limb by limb, my body would begin to unwind. I would slowly inhale, and then, as I exhaled, I would feel a wave of relaxation run through my body. Slowly, step by step, my conscious mind would begin to relax.

PSI World had given me a technique to tap into my subconscious and ultimately go beyond to my superconscious or spiritual level. Each time I centered, I learned that there were no limits within my mind's eye. I could use centering to explore my inner world, to harvest all of my ideas and inspirations and truly create my destiny.

Deep within my inner levels, I could summon anyone into my mental "workshop" and ask them questions. I had an elevator in my workshop and whenever I wanted to talk to someone, I just pushed the elevator button, the door would open, and they'd walk out. On this particular morning, my elevator was crowded. I pushed the button and out walked Jesus Christ, Mahatma Ghandi, and Martin Luther King, Jr.

Jesus was dressed in glowing white from head to toe. He had dark brown skin, long, black "woolly" hair, and his eyes were a colorless, bright white. An aura of light surrounded him and filled the entire room. I felt its warm glow against my skin. As he approached me, I quickly covered my eyes. His light was so blinding that nothing else was visible. I fell forward on my knees, completely overwhelmed.

"Oh Lord," I said, "thank you for coming to talk to me. I want so very much to change my life and help my people, but I have doubts and so many questions."

He didn't speak.

But I heard him.

Jesus told me to trust him one day at a time for guidance and answers. He said that my current money, career, and relationship troubles were a test of my faith and that I must persist in my goal of helping African American boys and that all my answers would be revealed. Then, before I could ask any more questions, the light faded and he was gone. With my head bowed and crouched on my knees, I looked up. The elevator was empty, the room, silent. I started to rise and suddenly felt a hand under my right arm, gently lifting me to my feet.

When I opened my eyes, I quickly rose from my chair and turned around, searching for something, anything to give credence to what I had just experienced. But everything was just as it had been before. I sat back down. A feeling of complete serenity and stillness came over me, and then, whatever fear or doubts I had were gone.

My apartment was still and very quiet. Suddenly I heard a loud screech outside. I looked out the window and saw a yellow school bus come to a lurching halt at the stop sign in front of my apartment. Inside the bus, I could see the ebony faces of African American boys and girls. They seemed to be yelling at the bus driver, who was angrily shouting over his shoulder back at them. The kids seemed to be chanting something at the driver, happily taunting him. I looked at his face and saw pure anger and hatred snarl from his lips. If I read his lips right, he shouted something like, "Sit down and shut the fuck up!"

I watched as the noisy bus, the tormenting kids, and the angry bus driver made their way through the intersection, up the hill and around the corner, until they were out of sight.

It was a sad sight. I thought of all of the other images of pain I'd seen on the faces and bodies of black people over the years—the homeless man down the street, pushing his life in a shopping cart; the tired and worn-out prostitutes of San Pablo Avenue; the familiar sight of young black men being handcuffed and placed in the back seat of a police car; the young brothers hanging out in front of Pon's liquor store in West Oakland, waiting for trouble. These and a lifetime of images rushed through my mind and I heard myself say—If there is one race of people badly in need of therapy, it's got to be the Africans here in America. We've experienced so much pain, poverty, and hopelessness, it's hardened our hearts. It's kept us from truly coming together.

I thought about my own transformation and what that had worked for me. Then it hit me. Suddenly it was clear to me that, if I was ever going to help African American boys, I must first help African American men learn to heal themselves, so they could be productive role models for boys. But how?

I had spent countless hours in the library reading books like *The Destruction of Black Civilization* by Chancelor Williams, *Living Synergistically*, by Thomas Willhite, *The Mis-Education of the Negro*, by Carter G. Woodson, and many others. I'd researched and studied the Egyptian Mystery System and gained an appreciation for the ancient wisdom of my ancestors.

But even though I could intellectualize my theories about what black people needed, I still lacked the final piece to the puzzle. The one thing that would make African American men wake up and take a close look at who they were. What would they need, to believe they could create the reality they wanted?

I finally realized that life is based on one truth: We create the reality around us by our belief systems—by what we believe. And that comes from Jesus Christ: "As you believe, so shall it be done unto you." I sat there at the table and began scrawling notes on a piece of paper. Jesus said, "It is your faith that has healed you," and it all made sense. I understood it. We create our internal reality, and we are partners with God in creating our external reality.

I asked myself how we can take people who believe that they are victims of their environment, their circumstances, of the government, of other people, and of situations, and get them to change those beliefs. How do we get them to realize that they are co-creators of everything in their lives?

I knew if I could find a way to teach them to change what they believed about their circumstances, they would accordingly change their circumstances for themselves.

One morning I picked up the *Tribune* and saw an ad that said, "Computer Instructor Wanted: Must know WordPerfect and Lotus." It was at a local trade school called CareerCom College. It just so happened that I was an expert at WordPerfect and Lotus. But for some reason, since I'd worked at the airport, I had never thought about working with computers again. I called and scheduled an interview. The next day I went in and met with their director of education.

John Sorenson was a tall, white man with red hair. He was friendly and impressed. "Why were you working at the airport?" he asked.

"I had experienced some hard times and I had to get a job. I couldn't find anything else."

He didn't press the issue, but he checked my credentials. After a brief interview, he hired me.

"When can you start?" he asked.

"Next week," I said.

CareerCom was located in East Oakland, in the Eastmont Mall shopping center parking lot. Classes were held on the second floor of a two-story retail and office complex. The majority of the students were African American men and women. CareerCom was accredited and had many campuses all over the country.

The night before class, I stayed up very late, preparing my

lesson plan. When I arrived at the school the next morning, I expected to be greeted by an enthusiastic group of students, eager to learn computers. Instead, I quickly discovered that most of these students had severe learning difficulties, and serious attitude problems.

"Good morning! My name is Roland Gilbert and I'm going to prove to all of you just how simple computers really are," I started. The room was silent. I searched for a friendly face, but there seemed to be none. All I saw was a room full of disinterested people, slumped down in their chairs, with no intention of making it easy for me. I passed out the course outline.

"OK, let's take a look at what you're gonna learn. WordPerfect is really the easiest word-processing program out there and it's one that a lot of employers require... Who here is taking this class for a job?" I asked. A few people in the front raised their hands.

"The rest of you are here out of sheer love for computers, right?" I said.

"Hey man, the only reason I'm in this class is so I can get my certificate for my plumbing apprenticeship. Once I get that, I'm gone, Audi 5000 G!" said a serious-looking young brother.

"So, you're going to be a plumber, huh?" I asked.

"That's right. Everybody has to shit; I might as well make money from it!"

There were a few laughs in the back of the room where he was sitting. He was a light-skinned boy, no more than nineteen or twenty years old. He wore a gold nugget earring in his left ear and his hair was cut into a high-top fade, with three parts cut on the left side. He said he wanted to learn a trade as a "backup plan" in case he didn't make it as a rapper. That's what he really wanted to be. The only reason he was in class was because his mother was paying for it. I spent the first fifteen minutes of class getting to know this angry young man. We talked while everyone else listened.

"By the way," I questioned, "what's your name?"

"Rudy, man, RUDY! What is this? 'Twenty Questions?'" he asked.

I guess every class has one student like that. The problem

was, I had several. And they weren't just enrolled in one of my classes. They were in all of them. I hadn't expected this kind of mentality. After all, this wasn't high school and *they* were paying for the courses. But, as I quickly discovered, most of these people had been borderline high-school students—if they had even graduated at all. Some only had G.E.D.s. But, regardless of their educational background, one thing was very clear— they all wanted out of the ghetto. And a trade or vocation that didn't cost a lot and didn't require four years of college was an easy, legal way out.

But their biggest problem was attitude. Many of them had a really defeatist, victimized, angry attitude about everything. That was my biggest challenge. I had to help them learn to overcome their own negative attitudes. They felt very poorly about themselves and they didn't even know it. Some had tried to go to junior college and failed, so they had come to CareerCom to learn a skill.

Most of the teachers thought the students were stupid. They weren't really interested in teaching or helping the students learn because they were too busy getting caught up in power struggles with them. Some even had to have security guards come into their classrooms to remove students.

My experience has taught me that "whatever I resist, persists." So, when conflicts arose in my class, I gave no resistance. I don't think it was any coincidence that I got a job teaching people who were considered difficult to teach. Each day was a true test of what I'd learned during the PSI World seminar. I just gave them love and used every opportunity to get them to see how smart they really were. This principle of being able to change negative belief systems had worked so well in my life, I knew I could teach it to them.

My greatest success came with a young lady in my WordPerfect class who was very scared of learning. Carmen was an attractive, young Mexican girl with a beautiful smile. She always tried hard in class, but for all her effort she could never complete her assignments. By the middle of the term, she was failing miserably. I knew if I didn't help her turn it around she'd flunk.

"Carmen, are you happy with your progress in this class?" I asked.

"Not really, but as long as I pass... that's enough for me," she said.

"Can I talk with you after class?" I asked.

Later, as everyone was leaving, Carmen walked up to my desk.

"Mr. Gilbert, please don't drop me from this class, I need it for my Travel Agent Certificate. I know I can catch up if you just give me a chance—I really have difficulty learning new things," she said.

Her last words echoed in my mind.

I'd heard it from many students. They'd say, "I can't do this or that or I'm not good at such and such."

The students were different, but the message was always the same. At some point in their lives, someone had told them that they had difficulty learning.

"Take this finger and put in on that key," I said.

She gave me a funny look and then pointed her index finger down onto the Escape key.

"Did you have difficulty in understanding that?" I asked.

"Of course not," she said.

"Good, now take these two fingers, hold these two keys down, and press the letter L."

She did it.

"Great! Now take this finger and put in on that key."

She did, and the "prompt" appeared on the screen. The screen cleared, and then a list of files rolled down from the top of the screen.

"Did you have difficulty understanding that?"

"No—but I don't know what I just did either."

"You just completed a new sequence of key commands for listing items in a file. It's that easy. Carmen, learning *is* 'not knowing what you're doing.' If you knew already, you wouldn't have to learn it, would you?" I asked.

"I never thought of it like that," she said.

"If you'll trust me and believe in yourself, learning will *happen* as a result," I said.

After that I tutored Carmen three days a week for the rest of the term and I got her to learn one key-stroke at a time. I found myself teaching her more about her belief systems and what she could do to change them than about WordPerfect itself. By the end of the term, she had turned her grades completely around. In fact, she became so enthusiastic about computers, she enrolled in my Lotus class the next term, "just for fun."

I taught four classes a day. By 2:30 p.m., I'd be through teaching my last class, leaving me plenty of time to develop my Simba idea. I still had the names and phone numbers of the brothers I'd met at the Kunjufu meeting and I got in touch with them. I had decided that the time was right. I would call them and invite them to an orientation meeting to tell them about my idea. If they were still as dedicated to the black community as they had said they were at that meeting, I knew I could get them to support my idea for Simba.

I also ran an announcement in the church bulletin about a need for African American men to work with boys. I distributed flyers and confirmed the meeting with all of the brothers who had been at the Kunjufu workshop. I set up the orientation at CareerCom, where I was able to get a classroom. I scheduled the orientation for 6 p.m. on a Monday evening.

Of the twelve men who had been at the workshop, only four showed up. About eleven other men had heard by word-of-mouth. I had assembled a row of about twenty-five chairs in the room, and as the men came in, I had them fill out a list with their name, address, and phone number. I took my place up front, where I had an easel with a big flip chart, some magic markers, and a few hand-outs.

"I'm Roland Gilbert. I want to thank you all for coming—if I told all of you that your cars were on fire *right now*, what would you do?"

No one said anything.

I walked over to the window, looked out and yelled, "Your cars are burning up, look! If you don't go out there right now and put the fire out, they'll be gone forever! What are you going to do?" I asked.

Still no one spoke up.

I singled someone out. "Brother, what kind of car do you have?"

"A Honda Accord," he said.

"What would you do if you looked out that window and saw it on fire?" I asked.

"I'd run out there and try to put it out," he said.

"Right! Sure you would... It's your car and you care about

it, right? Well, gentleman, I'm here to tell you that our children are on fire! They're burning up! And if they don't get our help they're going to continue to burn up and burn out!"

Then I laid out all of the statistics: "Did you know that one in four black males will have some contact with the criminal justice system before they reach eighteen years of age? Over half of all African American children grow up in a single-parent home and 50 percent of all African American children under six years old are living in poverty right now," I said

I pointed to a pie chart on the easel. "Here in Alameda County, the population is only 20 percent African American, but 65 percent of all males in Juvenile Hall are African American boys. Right here in Oakland, over 48 percent of all African American families are female-headed households. The number-one killer of African American males ages fourteen to nineteen is the hand gun. My brothers, what's going on?"

I could tell they were shocked by the statistics. Looking at each and every one of them, I asked, "Black men, where are you? What happens to these black boys when they grow up? What do they do with all of the anger, fear, and rejection that society dumps on them? Many, 'quite naturally' go to prison and become modern-day slaves," I said.

Then I told them about my idea for a Simba program. I described the Simba concept, explaining that it was a Swahili term that meant "lion," and that it stood for a concept developed in Africa, whereby men trained boys. "In Africa, an entire village raises a boy, not just his parents," I explained. "We have to continue that tradition."

Everything was going fine and they were buying into what I was saying. Then I told them that they'd have to complete an intensive sixty-six-hour training session before they would be able to work with the boys.

"What's the training for?" asked one man.

"It's a way for the men to come together and learn to be better leaders of self. They then pass on that knowledge to the boys," I said.

"Well, sixty-six hours is a long time, and I think most of us are already good leaders. I mean, that's why we're here, right?" He looked around for confirmation from the other men. A few nodded their heads in agreement.

The one speaking was a brother who had attended the

Kunjufu workshop. He was already aware of the statistics and had said he wanted to help, but he had some questions about my intentions.

"Roland, my brother. It looks like you've thought this program through. And we all know that the black male is Public Enemy Number One in the minds of white America. Black folks *do* need to come together so we can turn things around. I think the only way we can do that is to separate and take care of our own," he said.

"Brother before we discuss solutions to the problem, let's first agree to get together for this training," I said.

He looked at me as if he hadn't heard a word I said.

"Brother, you're not *listening*," he said emphatically. "We don't need to waste time in training when our boys are out there dying!"

I let him finish, then I simply said, "This is the way it's going to be. Simba is a program for all of us—men and boys. Those of you willing to sacrifice a little of your time to save some lives, please sign up on this sheet."

I passed a sheet around the room. The brother I had had the discussion with got up and walked out.

He was the kind of brother who always talked about unity for the black man, but he didn't know how to handle his own stuff, his own resentments, his own preconceived ideas. And so the thing he professes is not the thing that he did. It always saddens me whenever black people, sitting down in one room, trying to put their heads together to uplift our race, can't come to agreement—when ego and attitude rise up and prevent unity.

One of the crucial things I had to accomplish in that meeting was the concept that—If you can't make this date that we agree on, then you can't be involved in Simba.

I was putting myself out on a limb, but I was not going to fall into the trap of waiting, of being a victim to other peoples' agendas. Whoever agreed to the training, no matter who or how many, that's who I was going to work with. That was my leap of faith.

We set the date, September 1, 1988. The first forty hours of training would be held at CareerCom, from 6 p.m. to midnight Wednesday through Friday, and from 9 a.m. to 9 p.m. on Saturday and Sunday. Everything was set. Now all I had to do was be ready when the time came.

During those early days of Simba, I wouldn't have made it

without my present wife, Alyce. She was my rock and my support and still is. We met at a Sunday school training course at Allen Temple Baptist church in 1986. She had, and has, a wonderful, quiet innocence and inner beauty. After a few months we developed a casual, friendly, church-going relationship. I was attracted to her, but at the time I was celibate, and I was too busy getting my life together to be chasing women.

Besides, Alyce was married.

Then, one Sunday morning in November 1987, I went to the early morning service at church because I knew I had to go shopping later that day to get a birthday present for my daughter—*the very same daughter who only two years earlier had walked into my life from out of nowhere.*

In 1985, I had received a call from a young woman who claimed to be my daughter. After listening to her voice and what she had to say, I was very intrigued, and decided to meet with her. When we met face to face, there was no doubt in my mind. I had a twenty three-year-old daughter out there and I hadn't even known it. As we got to know each other, the most painful experience came when she finally asked what had happened—she wanted to know if I had really abandoned her. I explained to her that I hadn't even known that she had been born.

At fourteen years of age, I had already been in a lot of "relationships," and her mother had never told me she was pregnant. Her mother, or more than likely her grandmother, had decided to keep the information from me.

Now that I look back on it, they denied me the responsibility that I should have faced—the opportunity to learn responsibility at a young age. It was a classic case of black women stepping in and "loving" their sons while "raising" their daughters. If we as black men are ever to become responsible, loving adults, then our grandmothers and mothers will have to start holding us accountable for what we do, just as they do with young black women.

Over the next two years, my daughter and I found a way to develop a friendship, a relationship even, as father and daughter. It was incredible. There are no accidents. God brought her to me when he knew I'd be able to handle it. Had she called on me a few months earlier, I probably would have been too high on crack to care who she was.

As I walked out of the church that Sunday in November, I ran into Alyce. We started chatting, and I told her about my plan to go to the mall and pick out a gift for my daughter.

"I don't really know what to get her. I need a woman's opinion. Would you please come and help me?"

"Sure, I'd be happy to."

We left her car at the church and took my car. I had known Alyce for about a year, but for some reason I really began to notice her that day we drove down to Stanford. I had always liked her personality and we laughed a lot whenever we saw each other at church. Through our conversations and our body language, it was clear that we were attracted to each other.

We laughed and joked all the way to the mall.

I told her about my past relationships, my marriages, and my family.

She told me about her marriage, which was very sad. Her husband was very distant and she was lonely. He was much older than she, somewhere in his sixties, I think. He had become engrossed in his work and had never spent any time with her. She said she had tried to get him into marriage counseling, but he wouldn't go. She thought she wanted out, but she didn't know how to go about it. She was ambivalent.

We wandered through the mall, half looking for a gift, half looking at each other.

I took her back to her car at the church. We both knew we were going to see each other again, we just didn't know how. She had to call me; I couldn't call her. I got her work number and she had my number. So we began the "what are we going to do" phase of our relationship. The facts were clear. She "really liked" me and I "really liked" her, and we wanted to see each other. But she was married and it didn't seem likely that her husband would agree to a divorce. And she was unclear if she was even ready to get divorced herself. Emotionally it was very confusing.

After that day at the mall, I kept in touch with Alyce, but I continued to remain focused on my own self-growth and my plans for Simba.

When the day finally arrived, ready or not, I was going through with my plans for the Simba Leadership Workshop. I had reserved one of the largest rooms in the school and had a lot of work to do. I moved all of the furniture back to make an arc and placed several brown folding chairs precisely into a half-circle. I covered the windows so no one could look into the room from the hallway. Then I covered the clock and took various bulletins, flyers, and posters off the walls—it's very important that there are no visual distractions during the workshop.

I looked at my watch. It was 5:00 p.m. The men were due to arrive at 6:00 p.m. I figured I'd have just enough time to finish setting up the room, cue the music on my boom box, and hang the signs on the door and out in the hallway. I had all the items necessary for the workshop: flip charts, pens, notebooks, cassette tapes, name tags, and my notes. The signs I had made read, "WARNING... Workshop in Progress. Please Do Not Disturb."

It was difficult trying to get everything set up and also be mentally ready to present my program. Now, I have Simba instructors who help teach and set up the workshop, but on that first day, I was on my own. Once I had the room prepared, I closed and locked the door and sat down in the middle of the room. I had about forty-five minutes before the workshop began. I spent a lot of time centering myself, getting focused. Then, I got up, opened the door, and waited to see who was going to show up. I was very anxious. A lot of things were going through my mind. Would anyone show up? Would they all be late? How late would they be? How would I handle it?

They were late, but by 6:15 p.m. they had all arrived and as the last one entered I closed the door and asked them to get their name tags and take a seat. I had fifteen rules for participation in the workshop. I went over them and made sure everybody agreed to abide by them.

These men didn't know what was going to happen. They didn't understand that they would create the workshop themselves. The magic wouldn't come from me, it wouldn't come from the material—it would come from them. After everyone had gotten acquainted, I told them that in the following workshops, we were going to do a centering exercise. I explained it would enable them to tap into their deeper levels of consciousness, where their real power lies.

As I continued my presentation, using the flip chart and outlining certain metaphysical and psychological concepts, I could tell a few of the brothers were suspicious about what was being presented.

One brother in his early thirties began to ask questions about things that had nothing to do with what we were talking about. He wore glasses, sported a goatee, and was dressed in traditional African clothing. And he didn't really want to ask questions, he wanted to make statements. He would say things like, "Yes, I agree with what you're saying, and that's why the tyranny of the white man is so devastating. What we've gotta do is liberate our people's minds. Get them to throw off the mental shackles of slavery... to call out the devil white man for over four hundred years of oppression!"

Some of the brothers nodded in agreement, others just stared at him. I reminded him of the rules and said, "Thank you for your sharing, Jamal."

That first night everything went smoothly. The group dynamics were very interesting. Eight men had shown up, all with very different perspectives and backgrounds. There was a policeman, three probation officers, a mortgage banker, a lawyer, a musician, and a college student. As a group of black men, they shared many common experiences—childhood poverty, absentee fathers, mis-education about African people, and many other childhood scars. Still, they were very diverse in their views. Their religions ranged from Islam to Christianity and their ages ranged from twenty-three to fifty-eight years.

By the end of the night, it had become quite clear that my greatest challenge would be to bring all of these different types of black men together. Finally, I asked them to form a circle and hold hands. I played a song on the tape player and told them to listen to the words. When it was over I said, "See you tomorrow, on time and in agreement."

The next day one of the men was late. I told them that I would close the door at exactly 6:00 p.m. and if they couldn't make it on time, they wouldn't be able to continue the workshop. At 6:00 p.m. I taped my "Do not Disturb" sign on the door, and closed and locked it. About fifteen minutes into the workshop, I heard a few light taps on the door. I ignored them and continued with the workshop. When I opened the door at the break, I found a note taped to the door.

It read:

Dear Roland, I apologize for being late. I guess I didn't

realize how serious you were when you said "6.00 p.m." I wasn't able to free up my calendar this week and I figured I'd be able to make it here a few minutes late each night, and it wouldn't be a big deal. Guess I was wrong! Last night's material was so powerful, I was really looking forward to tonight. Please let me know when your next workshop will be held.

Sincerely, Charles Gregory

I used Charles as an example to the men. "It just so happens that our theme for today is '100 percent Commitment vs. Agreement.' You all agreed to be here on time and seven of you made it. Whatever each of you had to go through to get here is irrelevant. The fact is you're here because saving black boys is important to you... your word is important to you. We must stop blaming other people, events, or external circumstances for our failures. There are no excuses, only results. Only when we take full responsibility for how we think, feel, and act, can we truly grow and get everything we deserve out of life," I said.

I then explained the concept of centering and told the men that they were about to get about three hours' worth of rest in only fifteen minutes. I explained that they would not sleep, but that they would simply relax their minds. I showed them how to sit and position their bodies, then I turned on the tape player and turned off the lights.

It was the first time I'd ever shared this concept with a group. I wasn't sure they'd buy it. Except for the voice of the instructor on the tape, the room was completely silent. While the room was still dark, I heard the squeak of someone's chair. I opened my eyes and saw someone get up and walk to the door and stand there. It was Jamal, the brother who had commented about the "devil" white man the night before. I had been observing him throughout the workshop and I could tell he was very suspicious of what I was teaching.

He stood at the door with his arms folded across his chest and impatiently tapped one foot. It was important that I didn't let anything interrupt this exercise, so I remained very still, closed my eyes, and continued to center. If I got up now and tried to reason with Jamal, I would distract the other men.

All of a sudden the lights blinked on. "This is a form of mind control! What you're doing here is you're trying to brainwash us and get us under your control!" Jamal shouted. He was standing by the door, one hand on the light switch, the other on the door knob.

Nobody said a word.

I got up, turned the tape player off, and then sat back down in my chair. Then, quite calmly, I said, "Mind control? Jamal, what are you saying? Who has control of your mind?"

"I do... that's why I can see what you're trying to do. But it won't work. I don't want to lose my mind to you!"

"Jamal, why don't you sit down and join the group?"

"Look, you claimed this is about helping black boys get out of the ghetto, but so far all we've done is talk about ourselves and listen to some white man on a tape player talk about the inner levels of the mind. What about the children?"

I started to question him, and as I did, I discovered that he had a lot of emotional problems leftover from his childhood. He was afraid of the workshop's intentions, which asked that every participant seriously examine his childhood, his current beliefs, and his thinking patterns. I stood up and continued questioning Jamal. The guy was on automatic pilot. Verbalization was one way he protected himself. When he got afraid, he would begin to talk to cover up his fear.

"Do you think that the president of the United States is controlling your mind?" I asked.

"He tries to."

"On your job, do you think that people are controlling your mind?"

"I don't work!"

"What do you do?"

"I'm on disability."

"Are you under any kind of medical care?"

"I see a doctor occasionally."

I immediately stopped questioning him and called a break. During the break, I asked him to stay for a minute. We sat down in the back of the room, and soon I found out that he was seeing a therapist. He had been molested as a child and he was still dealing with it.

"Our children need our help. Our people are in pain and we all need to be healed," he said.

His eyes were glassy. It pained me to listen to him, and when he was finished "testifying," I said, "I want to thank you so much for coming and wanting to help our children, but I believe right now, because of the psychological problems you're having and the therapy you're receiving, it would be better for you not to participate with us."

He immediately agreed and understood.

"OK," he said, completely relieved.

When the other men came back, he was gone.

By 1:00 a.m., I was wrapping up the first night of the workshop. Only six men remained, and I needed at least that many to establish a functioning Simba chapter. If just one more dropped out, I'd have to stop the whole workshop. Questions ran through my mind. Would the remaining men stay around long enough to get it? Could I get them to resolve their ideological differences and learn to work together for the benefit of African American boys?

The next three days of the workshop would be the toughest.

Chapter 5

The I AM

There's no better way to gauge a man than by his results.
This is often harsh, but always fair.

During the two-year period before I started Simba. I had struggled to change my life. Many people helped me along the way, but it wasn't until I grasped the concept of the "I am," that I really began to take control of my life.

This concept is very simple. The I am is the foundation for all other human concepts known to man. Mahatma Ghandi understood this when he said, "Man is the center of a circle that has no circumference." He knew that the only limitations we have are the ones we create.

Centuries before Ghandi, our African ancestors, the Kemites (ancient Egyptians), centered their society and culture around the I am. I knew that the I am was the most crucial thing for the men to learn. Only then would they be able to realize that they didn't have to be victims of poverty, low self-esteem, poor living conditions, and of their own negative thinking, all of which was keeping them from fully realizing their true potential as African American men.

Most people's concept of I am is descriptive. They will say, "I am a police officer." "I am a doctor." "I am six-two." "I am 185 pounds." "I am happy." "I am depressed," and so on.

I could ask a hundred people and I'd hear the same thing, only in different versions; the reality is they are all saying the same thing. They're saying, "My existence lies within this little tiny circle and although my circle has a few different things in it, it's about the same size as everybody else's circle."

But the I am is about true liberty. When a man understands this, he becomes a leader. His thoughts, words, and actions will always be positive and he will always be internally motivated. He will fully accept responsibility for his own thinking.

When a man understands the I am, he becomes a leader of self.

This concept, though simple, is the hardest to teach. If a man is not ready to look at himself, to let his guard down long enough to learn something about the way he thinks, he is lost. For Saturday's session, I planned to use some rituals that would teach the men about the I am.

Saturday morning I arrived at the school at about 6:30 a.m. The room was empty except for six chairs in the center of the room, a metal waste basket, and a long desk and chair in the back of the room. A beam of morning sunlight broke through the blinds of the window behind me and lit up the room.

I arranged six chairs in a semi-circle in the front of the room. Completing this, I sat down in the back of the room and began to meditate.

Shortly before 9 a.m., all but one of the men were present. When the alarm on my watch beeped, signaling exactly 9 a.m., I got up and closed and locked the door. I turned the lights off, turned on the tape player, and sat back down to begin the centering exercise with the men.

When we finished the centering, I flicked the lights on and opened the door.

"Come on in, brother. You don't want to miss today," I said.

"Thank you, brother. I didn't think you'd let me in," said the brother who had been sitting outside.

He came in and sat down in the one empty chair within the half-circle. I walked to the front of the room and sat down next to the flip chart. The first sheet of paper on the flip chart had the words "Self-Honesty is the Key" written in small black letters in the middle of the paper.

"Charles, will you please stand," I said.

Charles, the brother who had been late, looked at me, then at the other brothers, let out a heavy sigh and slowly rose from his chair.

"Why did you choose to be late this morning?" I asked.

"What are you talking about? I didn't 'choose' to be late. I was late because of my brother. I went to check on him because he wasn't answering his phone this morning. I wanted to make sure he was going to make it here on time today," he said.

Everyone in the workshop had been assigned a "brother"

on the first day—to have someone to get support from. I had paired them up to inspire accountability and brotherhood.

I stood up and began to circle the arc of chairs and men, always keeping direct eye-contact with Charles while questioning him.

"But that's not the reason you're late. You chose to be late this morning and you chose to break your agreement with me and with your brothers," I said.

"But I was trying to support my brother. His car broke down and I knew he'd need a ride. I didn't choose to be late," he said.

"Well, were you here on time?" I asked.

"No, I wasn't!" he said angrily.

All of the other men were looking up at him and I could tell he was getting angry and frustrated. He felt I was putting him on the spot and he was starting to get very upset.

At the start of the workshop all of the men had agreed to follow certain rules of conduct throughout the training. One very important rule was that the men remain inside of the arc of chairs unless instructed otherwise. They also had to keep their arms at their sides and remain stationary while standing and talking. This allowed for open expression and prevented them from hiding behind habitual hand and arm gestures while speaking. As I watched Charles, I knew he was struggling.

By now I was standing directly in the middle of the half-circle. Looking him right in the eyes, I began to slowly inch my way closer to him.

"Judging by *results*, Charles, you just said 'Fuck it! I'll just be late and they'll understand.' Right?" I asked.

Now he was mad. He stepped out of the arc and came at me, yelling. "Now wait a goddamn minute! You told me I'm supposed to care about my brother; now you tell me I'm supposed to leave him behind so I can be here on time? What kind of bullshit is this?" he shouted.

He was up in my face now, still shouting.

"What do you want from me? What is this!?"

The other men were still sitting, quietly watching. They were obviously not going to get in this. I backed up a bit.

"This is about you, Charles. What's coming up with you... How do you feel?" I asked calmly.

"Pissed off, what do you think!" he said.

I continued to ask him questions about how he felt and why he was *choosing* to be angry. I never tried to make him wrong or take control of the discussion. Instead I gave him love, which diffused his anger. This was the key in keeping things from getting physical. I got him to see that his brother hadn't made him late. I told him that blaming his lateness on his brother's situation or becoming angry over my questions was taking away his power. I explained that he always had a choice, no matter what the external circumstances were. It was his choice to handle the situation the way he did. We went over several other ways he could have handled things differently, so that he could have still kept his word, without becoming a victim to his brother.

Each night after the workshop, I would give the men assignments to complete by the next day. The assignments usually required them to do some introspection on what they had learned and then to record it in their journals.

"OK, brothers. Let's check your lifework," I said.

All but one brother had finished the assigned task. He had left his notebook at home.

"Vernal, who is your brother?" I asked.

"Joshua."

"Joshua, will you please stand? Did you check on Vernal this morning to see if he had brought his lifework?" I asked.

"No, I didn't," he said.

"Why?"

"He didn't say anything about it to me," he said.

The main point of the entire workshop is to teach African American men how to come into agreement, how to work together for the benefit of our people. My intention was to get them to think as one group, with six movable parts. Any trace of egotism or irresponsibility would ruin the whole process.

But they still didn't get it.

"Well, you're going to take some time to ask yourself why it was not important to you to offer your support to your brother," I said.

Then I asked Joshua a series of questions and tried to get him to see that his thinking was detrimental to the unity of the group. Slowly he began to see my point. But as a group, they were still out of agreement. They had to all complete each task together or they couldn't move on. They had to come together.

"You are out of agreement with me, with yourselves, and this workshop. This workshop stops right here, right now, until you can come into agreement. I'll be outside. Come and get me when you're in agreement," I said.

I picked up my things and walked out of the room.

Two hours later, I checked on them, and found that they were still out of agreement. I left again. I had told them they had to come into agreement and solve the problem together, and that they could not leave the room, except to come get me. They couldn't figure out how to get Vernal's lifework done without leaving the room to get the needed supplies.

They were stumped. As I sat outside the door, I could hear them arguing.

I sat wondering if they would ever get it together and realize that they had everything they needed to solve their problem right there in the room. But they were too caught up in the "how-to" part of the problem. They still didn't understand that the "how-to" part was secondary. What they had to agree on was the "to do" part. Once they had their intentions clear and had decided what to do as a group, the mechanism, or the way to do it, would naturally follow.

After fifteen minutes or so the door opened. "Roland, we are in agreement and we'd like to continue the workshop," said Charles.

"You are, huh? OK, let's continue." I got up and walked back into the room. "How did you come into agreement?"

"Since Vernal can't go out and buy the required supplies to complete his lifework, each of us agreed to do yesterday's lifework over and turn it in tomorrow at the same time he turns his in," said Rashid, the youngest member of the group. "That way we will all be in agreement," he added.

"That was a pretty long assignment—and you'll be getting another one tonight. You're willing to do it all over for Vernal's sake?" I asked.

"Yes," they said in unison.

"You're willing to become victims to Vernal's irresponsibility?" I said.

Nobody said anything. Obviously they hadn't looked at it like that. They thought they were supporting Vernal.

"Get creative, gentleman. You don't have to set yourselves back in order to help your brother. The answer to your problem is right here in this room."

Their eyes searched the room.

They looked at each other.

They looked at me. Then Vernal stood.

"Roland, all I need to complete my lifework is another notebook. Do you have any extra notebooks handy?"

"Sure, I do. Would you like to purchase one?"

"Yes."

I picked up a box sitting in the front of the class. The box was clearly marked "School Supplies," and it contained several college notebooks, pencils, pens, scissors, and so on.

"That'll be $5.00, please," I said.

They were dumbfounded. The box had been sitting in plain view all the time. They had just failed to recognize it as an answer.

"Brothers, if we just take the time to look within for our help, we can tackle any problem in life. You were so preoccupied with seeking external ways to solve this problem, that the solution sat right here under your nose and you failed to see it. And so it is with many of the problems our people face," I said. "Look within, and to each other. That's where our strength is."

The meat of the whole workshop was yet to come. It was the "processing," or the period when I asked them questions about their childhood, family, and personal life.

This was the most challenging part of the workshop because it asked the men to come face to face with the pain of their past. Each man had several "issues," or scars. The problem was, they weren't even aware of the damage these issues were doing in their lives. As black men, we've been taught not to bond. We are taught to be adversaries instead of allies, fighters instead of lovers. In a holistic sense, we never learn to be lovers of ourselves, lovers of our families, and lovers of our culture. Getting black men to expose their feelings about childhood scars and adult pain in front of other men is the most crucial part of the workshop.

Each man had something in his life that was limiting him.

But they were unaware of it, and it was preventing them from realizing their true potential. Before they could be any good to the children, they had to "unlearn" many of the negative-thinking habits they had learned while growing up. Otherwise, consciously or unconsciously, they would pass all of their "stuff" onto the children.

By Sunday, the last day of the workshop, I was mentally and physically drained. It had taken everything I had to do the Leadership Workshop for the first time. I had prepared all of the study material myself and coordinated everything. Each day I was up before 6 a.m. preparing for the next day's session. From 8 a.m. to 4 p.m., I was in class, and by 6 p.m., the men would arrive for the workshop.

I was still not sure if the training had worked. The men had learned the material, but I wasn't sure if they were truly bonded. At the very last circle on Sunday, I asked them to hold hands and listen to the words of a song. After the song, the men finally hugged each other and I knew then that all my effort was going to pay off, that it—the workshop, Simba—was actually going to work.

Chapter 6

The Simba Six: The Men

A lot of what takes place in the Leadership Workshop is sacred. I cannot begin to describe the men's emotional and psychological experiences. For this reason, I'll let them tell you:

Michael Holland, 37, Oakland Police Officer
I was surprised about the sixty-six-hour training. I thought, Hey, I'm a police officer. I'm a responsible individual. What do I need to go through this guy's training for? But later I figured, OK, I'll try it. What do I have to lose?

After that first night, as I walked out, I made a conscious decision that no matter what I had to do that week, I was going to give all of my energy to try to learn everything I could. Those first six hours were overwhelming to me. What we were learning fit so well into all of the things that I understood about the failure of the criminal justice system and why society is going downhill. I had never gotten that much information, that clearly, that quickly, in my life. I've had a couple of psychology classes in college, and they didn't give me anywhere near as clear an understanding about why people function the way they do as this man did in the first six hours of the seminar. After the second night, I was a little intimidated but I was absolutely determined to come back and learn more about myself.

Here I was, a black man out there trying to help my own people, and they were totally rejecting me because sometimes I had to lock up some of my own people, even though they were the victims. So on the one hand, African American folks didn't want me to take other African American folks to jail, but they also wanted me to do something about the guys committing crimes against them. It was sort of a Catch-22, and it frustrated the hell out of me.

The story I like to tell is about a lady whose purse got snatched. This little old, African American woman was walking down the street I'm driving down, and I see this black dude come up and hit her, snatch her purse, and take off. She goes down. I jump out of my car and start chasing him. I'm chasing him through the projects and he goes around a corner and just disappears. He was only twenty feet in front of me and the buildings are two hundred feet long, so there's no way he made it to the other end. He ducked in one of the doors there. I tried to get folks to tell me. "Which way did he go? Which way did he go?" I asked. "Look, this guy just robbed a black woman right here out of your neighborhood. Which way did he go?"

They just stood there and said, "We ain't gonna help you lock a black man up." I was so frustrated by that incident that I asked my sergeant to move me to another beat.

When I went through the leadership workshop, I learned that being a responsible black man meant a hell of a lot more than going to work on time, bringing a paycheck home, paying all of the bills, and not going out and screwing around with other women. When you go through Simba, you learn how to take control of your destiny and help others take control of theirs.

I realized I had an anger "program." It was making me do a lot of drinking. I had gotten to the point with my wife where I felt like arguing didn't do any good, so I just shut up and bottled up all of my anger—which was slowly but surely destroying my marriage. As we continued the training, I got clearer about some of my issues—my self-esteem, my anger, my issues with women, and my fear issue. After the workshop, my relationship with my wife improved and I stopped getting as angry about things I couldn't control.

Simba is the opportunity to meet and get to know the most effective, powerful, and loving man you'll ever meet, and that's the person you see in the mirror everyday. Once you learn how to love, you start to live differently. The bottom line is this: When a man walks away from Simba, he learns how to love, even his enemies.

I think we're creating a new version of the "village" concept. I think there's an Ashanti saying that goes, "It takes an entire village to raise a child." What we're teaching men to do is to be the new village elders. Part of being a village elder for me is to teach—my son, the boys in Simba, I even teach Simba concepts to the officers in my squad, so that they can get an understanding of why a lot of people do what they do out there. There's nothing else in my life that's taught me to be in control of my life like Simba has. And I teach the boys what I've learned... what I'm living.

Rashid Shaheed, 32, Consultant

The workshop wasn't anything I expected. It was really a lot of good stuff and it was so personal. That first day, I was excited about the work Roland gave us. By the third day things were getting serious. Intense.

When I was growing up, there was a point where all my family (eleven children, one mother, no father) ate was bread and milk. That's it. We dipped the bread in the milk and that was breakfast, lunch, and dinner. We ate sugar-bread sandwiches and mayonnaise sandwiches. We had one of the smallest houses on the block and when it rained, we would put buckets throughout the house so the floor wouldn't get wet. The front porch was crumbling and broken down. It was definitely a state of poverty, and I internalized it. After going through Simba I learned that I had a poverty "program," which said, "All I need is a quarter, that's all I need. I don't need a hundred dollars, just give me a quarter, and I'll be all right."

Another issue I had during the workshop was the religious aspect. I had to ask myself, is Simba going against my religious teachings? I was the only Muslim brother in my chapter. Everyone else was Christian. The brothers never criticized me or made me feel out of place. We didn't promote our religion, and that was really a good dynamic. When I talk to Muslims about Simba, they say "This is Islam." The teachings are all about self. The Koran speaks about "know thyself" and it's in the African teachings of Kemet also. Simba just solidifies all of those teachings.

Since the seminar, I've learned not to think like a victim, not to blame external circumstances for why I'm feeling a certain way. I understand that certain things happen, but I don't have to let them run my life. Now I know that I am my best friend and that nobody else can determine how I feel unless I allow them to. I'm not going to be a victim. I've found my purpose: to teach African Americans, particularly the men and boys, not to think like victims.

Simba helped me to see where I was at, why I was getting the results I was getting in my life. I would tell myself I wanted one thing, but my "programs," my habitual ways of thinking, would cause me to react another way.

Simba has given me the ability to say that I am unique. To say that my creator has endowed me with the ability to succeed. It has given me more insight. The seminar allowed me to get real with myself and really check out what was happening with me. I think Simba is a superb way of liberating African Americans. No other program for African American boys trains black men to be leaders of self the way Simba does.

It would be a disservice for leaders to get out there and start teaching our boys and not be aware of their own negative programs.

Vernal Martin, 61, Probation Officer

I was born in Dayton, Texas, but I was raised in Houston. My mother died when I was five. I'm the youngest of seven children. I earned a degree in Sociology, and I've been married since 1965. I started working for the Alameda County Probation department in 1971.

When I first heard about the leadership workshop, my first reaction was that it was awfully long. I work long hours at work and I thought it was going to take up too much of my time. I didn't go along with it at first, because I didn't think it was necessary for me to help the boys.

On the first day of the workshop, I was late, and I had a lot of excuses as to why I was late. But my excuses weren't any good. He told us that if we gave our word we had to keep it. That the boys would learn from our actions, not from our words. He gave us books to read, and assignments to complete. After I went through the training, I accepted it enough to know that Simba was something I wanted to do. So I committed myself to do it for our boys. In order for us to help the kids, we had to have something to offer them. That workshop gave us something to offer.

When I was in my late twenties, I had auditioned for Count Basie's band. To my surprise, I was accepted, and when Basie left to go on a tour, he said he wanted me to start when he got back. Some of the guys in his band told me that the life of a musician was not all it was cracked up to be and that they would quit if they knew how to do anything else. Count Basie himself told me to think about it, because if I wanted to get married and start a family, I'd have to take into account the traveling lifestyle.

Soon I started making up excuses for why I shouldn't go. I finally came to the conclusion that I wouldn't. I thought I'd just continue singing in the local clubs. I guess I felt like I didn't deserve to sing with Count Basie's band—little ol' me, you know? That's where my low self-esteem came in. It wasn't until I started in Simba that I first talked about this. During the training I found out I had a low self-esteem. I had thought that I was fine. Roland told me that Count Basie was probably thinking that he would be fortunate to get me and there I was thinking that I was not good enough.

I often asked myself, What would it be like if I'd gone to sing with Count Basie's band? What would I be doing now? I guess I'll never know.

During the workshop, Roland gave us something to give to the boys. We needed to get rid of all of the negative programs that we'd learned over the years, so we wouldn't pass them onto the boys. That was the whole idea—having positive things to give to the boys. Simba is the very best program I've ever been in. I've learned things about myself that I probably would never have learned, and I learn things from the kids all the time.

Problems can be solved—we just have to believe we can do it.

We are the problem. Too many of us want somebody else to do it. We think we don't have time. I didn't think I had time, but now I make time. I leave here at 3:30 on Mondays and Wednesdays, I go pick up a little boy, and we go to Simba. I have a lot of work here, but what's more important, our boys or Alameda County's work? I'm doing this for our boys.

Charles Ransom, 50, Real Estate Broker
I'm from Detroit. I moved out to California to go to college. I graduated from San Francisco State with a B.S in Economics. I've been married for two years.

I went to the Workshop more out of curiosity and because Roland was bugging me to check it out. Roland and I were in

Sunday school class together, so it was kind of hard for me to duck him. At the time, I had just got my second divorce and I was somewhat searching for something to get involved in. I thought maybe this was an opportunity.

I wasn't really sure what to expect. But with all of my sales and management training, I had always been taught to go into a situation trying not to have any pre-conceived ideas. On the first day of the workshop, Roland gave us enough to make us want to come back.

When we learned about our emotional make-up, I learned that it was all right for me to be emotional. That it was nothing I should be ashamed of, or to try to hide. I've always been emotional and I used to be ashamed of it. One time when I witnessed a fight, I saw a man backhand a kid. The next thing I knew, the police and my friend were pulling me off the man. They had to take me off him because I was about to kill him. If I see somebody in a weak situation, I have a tendency to react. Or if I see a sad situation, I become emotional. The thing is, I can get emotional about anybody but me. When it comes to me, I'm detached.

We were all taught that a man should never show emotions and that a man should always be strong. I can remember as a child that I cried in church when my grandfather died. It was the first time someone close to me had died. My sister and I were crying at the church and my mother looked down at me and shook me and said, "You shouldn't be crying like this; this is not your father. You should be strong."

I got a lot from my mother. She was the matriarch of our family and she felt that she had to be responsible for everybody. I know some of that rubbed off on me. I feel I should be responsible [for everybody], and when I'm not, that's when my guilt comes up. I felt I was responsible for my divorces. I didn't deliberately set out to get divorced, it just happened. But the fact that it happened twice made me feel even more guilt. When I went through Simba, I gradually learned that I had a guilt complex, a guilt "program." The workshop made me realize that I wasn't responsible for my failed marriages. I had done the best that I knew how to do.

In the early days of Simba, before we got the boys, we were meeting every week, and we weren't getting paid. It was all unbelievable. It was amazing to me that when I got to the meetings, we'd all be there. I went because I felt a commitment to go and see it through, even though in the back of my mind, I still had doubts if we could pull it off. You could see that Roland was committed. You could see he had a purpose. That is the sign of a good leader—if you can see that the leader is committed, it helps you in your own commitment. He never missed a meeting. He was always full of purpose.

Simba is a long-term commitment to role-modeling for boys. It's something that you have to experience for yourself, and learn about your own negative programs, so that you can be in control enough to give the boys positive programs.

The main thing Simba did for me is make me understand who I am and why I do the things the way I do. I've had a lot of training in sales and everything, but that was more external, about how to deal with other people, not how to deal with myself. What are my weaknesses and my strengths? Most people are too afraid to even analyze themselves in that way. But you can't really grow until you know where you need to grow.

Joshua Nichols, 57, Probation Officer

I was born in Bunke, Louisiana, the ninth of twelve children. I grew up on a fifty-seven-acre farm with both my mother and father in the house.

I attended Southern University and graduated with a degree in Secondary Education. Right after college, I got a job teaching high school Social Studies for a year in Marksville, Louisiana. One day I took my class to a state park. When we got to the entrance of the park, there was a sign that read, "For Whites Only." I wanted to take my class through this park because it was a historical burial ground for American Indians. They wouldn't let us in the park. My class and I decided to go to the local courthouse and question this. Then people from the Sheriff's department came by the school and wanted to know who had told them about this. My kids said, "Our teacher, Mr. Nichols."

After that incident, I got tired of dealing with the prejudice and I decided to leave Louisiana, so I came to California in 1958. Shortly after that, I got a job with the Alameda County Probation Department.

After working in probation for over twenty years, I could see that there was a lot to be done. I couldn't do it on the job because there were certain constraints. But I felt there was something I could do to contribute other than sending kids to Juvenile Hall. Those kids needed somebody to get to them before they came to probation. At the Simba Orientation, I listened to what Roland was saying and I realized that was what I wanted to do.

When I first got to the leadership workshop I thought that this was maybe some form of brainwashing, but that I could deal with it because I knew I was only going to accept so much of it. But as time went on, I started to develop more confidence and trust. I realized Roland knew what he was doing. I thought that maybe something had happened to him earlier in his life.

The workshop was intense—only six of us made it out of the twenty or more men who came to the orientation. During the workshop, I learned that my issue was procrastination. I felt that maybe I could have done a better job with my two sons—my wife did most of the raising. I was raised by both my parents, but my father was sort of a quiet type, who didn't do that much talking. I guess I learned that from him when it came to my sons. But at the workshop, I learned that I was responsible for the way I think, feel, and act. And I'm not as judgmental as I was. I also learned that I don't have to get approval from anyone else.

The last day, when we were in the final circle, I felt a special bonding with all of the guys who had gone through the training. It was wonderful. Simba has helped me tremendously. This program is important because it's the only way we are going to help young black men survive. Simba will become the standard method for survival.

After the training we needed to recruit boys. At first we were a little reluctant to go down to the heart of West Oakland. But we did. We met at a community center in the Acorn Housing projects. Then we just started knocking on doors. We explained that we were starting an organization for boys who didn't have fathers and that we were going to train the boys. After we explained what we were doing the word kind of spread and then they started looking for us.

Donald Walker, 47, Probation Officer

I first learned about Simba through my friend Josh. He gave me some information about the Simba orientation and I decided to go through the leadership workshop. I was cautious about committing to a concept I didn't know much about.

During the workshop we talked about some childhood issues. My mother raised me. I was four years old when my father left, and I saw him for the first time as an adult when I was twenty-eight. The group went through a process where we presumably let go of all of that old "baggage," that anger. But even now, I still have to deal with the fact that he wasn't around and made no effort to really get involved with me at an early age. I was fortunate to have a stepfather who is still with my mother, and who is essentially my father.

My stepfather got together with my mother when I was ten. My grandfather was also around, but he had a drinking problem. When I saw my father as an adult, I recognized that he had a drinking problem, too. The conditions black men face in this society drive them to drink, and it continues to, generation after generation.

I talked about my mother and about how I felt that I hadn't spent time with her. She's still alive, thank God for that, but I had gotten so consumed with my own personal life that I just didn't spend enough time with her. It was real interesting to go through the training, because of that whole concept of putting your feelings out there and overcoming that instinct to not want to reveal yourself to people—to guard certain parts of yourself from others. It's simply a way of protecting yourself from being judged and being vulnerable.

I've always had a range of emotion that I would express, and after that I drew a line. There are not that many men that I could sit down with and get into very personal issues about childhood and fatherhood, and how those issues have affected me in my personal life. What was very clear, was that Roland was trying to define what commitments and agreements were. It was all about learning how to take responsibility for what we say we're going to do. I think when I make a commitment or just give my word to somebody, I'm more aware of that responsibility now than ever before, because it's something people do measure you by. I've always felt that I could pretty much be counted on, but I wasn't 100 percent reliable, and I'm still not, but I'm better.

I found myself dancing around things without really trying to get too revealing. It was all very sensitive and emotional for me. I found out that I expressed anger as a child by pouting, and that it had carried over into adulthood. When my wife and I had disputes, I would rarely raise my voice, but I would sulk or pout. I probably still do—I haven't worked that out all the way, but at least now I'm aware of it. When I came face to face with my "programs," fear came up for me. I saw some stagnation in my life, just plateaus and no real growth. I did a lot of talking but no doing—a lot of bullshitting myself. Fear was my program. Fear of failure and fear of judgment. Self-doubt. A man can spend his whole life hiding from himself, not knowing who he is. The workshop can not only help you find out who you are, but help you to go in a direction that you want to go. It's all really quite simple. It's taught me that living is a matter of starting from within and going outward. That's it in a nutshell. You can't take care of your family, you can't take care of all of your other responsibilities, if you can't deal with yourself.

The bond that developed between us in the workshop came out of everybody's willingness to share something so personal that you knew that they had to reach a level of trust to do that. And through the course of that training, we all came to respect and really care for each other.

I wanted to be part of Simba because I wanted to have an impact, to make a contribution, to make somebody's life better. After the workshop, I felt real charged. It opened up some doors for me in terms of the way I deal with life. Now, I think I'm a much better listener. The way I look at things and the approach that I take is pretty much a result of what I've learned through the Simba experience. I rank my experience in Simba in the top five of all my life experiences.

I can't help but think we've made an impact in the kids' lives, because they keep coming back. They come in the rain, they come when it's cold, they come when you least expect them to come. They could be doing a whole lot of other stuff out there. And it's not that what we're doing is all that special, but we're showing them—here are some men who are taking some time out of their lives to say, "Hey, what can we do to help you be the person you want to be?"

Chapter 7

The Johnsons

"Roland, this is Teena Johnson. She's going to be in our Sunday school class today," said Ola, my co-teacher.

The woman Ola introduced me to looked to be in her early thirties. She seemed uncomfortable, like this was her first time in church.

"Teena, welcome! We're glad to have you study the word with us," I said.

"Thank you" she said.

There was something different about her. Her mannerisms and demeanor were very guarded. She had a short, brown afro and a light-tan complexion. Her eyes were dark and heavy. She was attractive in a simple sort of way, but there was a deep sadness in her eyes that I'd seen before. Throughout the class, I kept noticing her eyes. She watched me and I watched her. Soon I could tell that she knew *that I knew* what was up with her. She had the same look I had when I was a crack addict. When you've been there, you can read it in a person. Their energy is different. By the time class was over, it was obvious to me that she had a "jones."

After class, I asked her some questions about herself, her situation. She was supporting three children on her own, was barely getting by. I thought the church would be willing to help out so I took her to see Deacon Little.

"Sure we can help," said Deacon Little. "Just fill out these papers and we'll get you something in a couple days."

"Is there any way we can get her something to take home to her children. They need some food today," I said.

"Well, the Benevolence Fund is only available from Tuesday through Saturday. It takes us at least two full days to process all requests and the offices are closed on Sunday."

We had come up against the church bureaucracy.

"Alright brother, here's her application. We'll just have to see what else we can do for her," I said.

They told Christ that he couldn't heal anyone on the Sabbath. Well, neither it seemed could the church give benevolence on Sunday. As I walked Teena down the hall and out into the morning sunshine, I couldn't help but think, What are we doing? We've gotten so far away from African tradition that the Eurocentric viewpoint even plagues the black church. European thinking always puts the organization before the people.

I drove her home in my old Datsun B-210. She owned a corner house by Eastmont Mall, on 65th and Bancroft Avenue. It was a two-story house with weeds and garbage all over the front yard. As we walked into the living room a small boy and a girl greeted us.

"Mommy, tell Monie to stop" said the little boy.

"She keeps copying me," he cried.

"She keeps copying me" mimicked the little girl.

"See, what I mean?" said the boy.

"See what I mean! What a little baby!" said the girl.

The kitchen area was filthy and the air smelled like an old, damp dish rag. There were dirty dishes, pots, and pans stacked in the sink. An old-fashioned stove sat in the corner with a long chimney-like pipe sticking out of it. The walls were smudged with children's fingerprints. Toys, shoes, and clothes were scattered all over the floor.

"Where's Jamila?—Jamila! Jamila!" shouted Teena.

"Yeah," cried a voice from inside the bathroom.

"I told you to do these dishes. Get out of that bathroom and get in this kitchen." Jamila had been talking on the phone in the bathroom and obviously hadn't anticipated her mother's return.

"Mom, I've been trying to get Robert and Monie to help me all morning. They don't ever help!" said Jamila.

"Teena, I need to run to the grocery store and I'm going to pick you up a few things." I said.

"Roland, you don't have to do that... Wait!" she shouted.

I turned and headed for the door.

"I'll be right back." I shouted.

Teena had her hands full—alone and raising three children: Robert (age seven), Monita (age ten), and Jamila (age twelve). She had divorced her husband six years ago because his gambling habit was destroying their marriage. Now she struggled to keep the house they'd bought together, to keep her children in private school, and to keep her job at the post office. On the ride to her house, she had confessed to being a crack user and I told her I had recognized her "look." I told her about my former crack addiction and that I could help her if she'd let me. She said she'd been up all night calling drug clinics for help, but only got recordings. She found Allen Temple in the phone book and decided to call.

When I got back to the house, Jamila was washing dishes.

I'd bought them the basics: flour, sugar, potatoes, cereal, milk, and a half-gallon of strawberry ice cream as a treat for the kids. I sat two brown paper bags on the table, smiled, and waved goodbye to Teena. She was on the phone.

"Hold on a minute Mama—Roland, I told you that..." she said.

"Teena, I'll call tomorrow to check on you, OK?" I said as I walked out the screen door and headed for my car.

After that, I began to develop a relationship with Teena and her family. On Sundays, I'd pick up her children and take them to church with me. Every year, Allen Temple held a big church revival and it was about to kick off. It ran from Sunday to Friday and many of Oakland's most renowned preachers, choirs, and musicians came to fellowship, rejoice, and save souls all week long.

On Friday night I decided to take Teena's son, Robert, with me.

When we got to the church, there was a long line outside and we could hear loud music and people singing. Inside, the pews were packed. Black folks of every size and shade swayed, clapped, stomped their feet, and sang praises to the Lord. Except for the very young and the very old, everyone was standing, which made it difficult for us to negotiate the pews. Eventually we squeezed down the aisle and found a space in the middle of the third pew on the left.

The choir was just finishing a song.

"Allen Temple! Allen Temple! Stand up and praise the Lord" said a deacon. "It's revival time!" he continued.

With a wave of his hand, the brother on the organ signaled

to the choir, then he hunched over the keyboard and fingered a few notes of "Hiding Place." The choir director lifted his arms and motioned to a sea of men and women cloaked in purple and gold robes. Women in the choir beat their tambourines, the organ rolled into a high-pitched melody, and the congregation lit fast into a quick hand clap.

"Y'all ready to have church?" shouted the deacon.

"Yes!" shouted the congregation.

"Then stand on your feet and put your hands together" he said. The choir sang out:

Where you gonna run to
On Judgment Day?
Run to the rocks just to hide your face.
Rocks will cry out, no hiding place.
Where will you run!
Where will you run!
On Judgment Day

Oh sinnerman, can hear him calling
Will you be ready?
On Judgment Day
He's coming back, He's coming back
On Judgment Day!

Where you gonna run to
On Judgment Day?
Run to the rocks just to hide your face.
Rocks will cry out, No hiding place.
I'm gonna be ready,
I'm gonna be ready,
Get Ready! Get Ready!

The choir sang with so much energy and love, the very presence of the Lord made the air crackle and the walls shake. Folks were falling out, getting happy, and dancing in the aisles. Ushers rushed back and forth trying to keep people from hurting themselves.

"Amen! Amen! Yes sir! The Lord is working in here tonight, isn't he? Praise him! Church, Judgment Day is coming soon and I'm gonna be ready! Will you? You know God has a plan.

His plan is salvation. Everlasting life! Hallelujah! For we know all men's hearts are evil, that all have sinned and fallen short of the glory of God. But our Lord is merciful. He sent his only begotten son to die on the cross for all of the world's sins," said pastor James, now in front of the pulpit.

"Praise him!" cried a woman with both hands lifted above her head.

"Amen!" said an elderly woman up front.

"Fathers look down at your sons—oh how you love them! How we all love our young, precious, beautiful, black boys! We try to lead them and train them up in the way they should go so that one day they can defy the odds against them and make it to manhood. Think of the *love* you have for your son—for those of you who have only *one* son—think of your precious love! Now think of the pain and sacrifice that God bore for you, for us, for the world and its sins!" said the pastor.

"Yes sir!" cried a woman. "Tell it!"

I looked down at Robert and smiled. He sat, wide-eyed, cautiously looking around the room. This was his first time in church and after watching me jump up and down and shout, I'm sure he thought I was crazy—or surely on my way.

"Church, Judgment Day is coming. Where will you stand? If you were to die today, do you know without a doubt that you'd be among the chosen? God is ready to clean us up, that we might all be lifted up to where we belong. When I speak of deliverance, I know of what I speak. The greatest high is not crack cocaine, it's not marijuana, it's not alcohol, but it's the Lord Jesus Christ. Amen! How many of you know that Jesus is real?" said the pastor.

Everyone in the church raised their hands.

"I don't know what your problems are today. I don't know what your situation is. You may be living on the streets of East Oakland, you may be unemployed, you may be struggling with drugs—whatever it is, bring it all to God right now. Bring it to the Lord. He'll fix it. This is an invitation to come. How many want the Lord to wash them? Who will come? The kingdom of heaven awaits..."

Slowly, one by one, teary-eyed men and women began to walk down the aisle. The pastor greeted them with open arms and they took their places behind him. The pastor stood with open arms.

"Who will come?" he said.

A father and son, then a single mother and her two children, then a young couple… all seemingly burdened, headed towards the pulpit.

I looked down at Robert. He was very quiet.

"Do you want to go, Robert?" I asked.

"Yeah," he said.

"Do you want me to go with you?"

"Yeah."

I took him by the hand and we took that long walk down the aisle.

When we got to the front, the pastor shook Robert's hand and gave him a hug. The pastor was always especially glad to have the opportunity to help save the soul of a young person. He was grinning and very happy. The following week, on Easter Sunday, eight-year-old Robert Johnson was baptized, accepting Christ as his Lord and savior.

For several weeks to come, I continued to pick up Teena's children and take them to church. Sometimes she would go. Eventually, her other two children, Monita and Jamila, were baptized and they too joined the church. For awhile, Teena came with us. She attended Sunday school and Bible study. But she never got baptized. She had an issue with the image of Christ. I explained spiritual concepts to her, that Christ wasn't a white man with blue eyes and long hair. But she still wasn't ready. She did begin to make progress though. She stopped smoking crack. And I began to work with her, taking her to Cocaine Anonymous meetings and helping her whenever she needed me. For about two months straight, Teena was at church every Sunday. Then in December, she just stopped coming.

When I asked her children about her, they just said she had locked herself in her room and had stopped going to work. They said they only saw her when she came out to cook, or when she went to the bathroom. I called her but she never returned my calls. Weeks later, when I found out the kids were staying with their grandmother, and that she had lost her job at the post office where she had worked for over ten years, I knew what was up.

One Friday night, without calling, I dropped by her house. I found her sitting on the porch, looking anxiously up and

My father, Maurice Gilbert, circa 1943.

My father circa 1930.

My high school graduation photo,
1965, 17 years old.

Me around 15 months old, just
starting to walk, with my older
brother Maurice looking on.

Me with my wife Velma at Caesars Palace in Las Vegas, Nevada. I am 19 years old and celebrating my first successful bank robbery.

My cousin Harold Williams, who helped me sneak into The Broadway nightclub, and was my mentor in the "fast life."

Milford Lewis and "Squirt," 1981. *Credit: Marlene Sandeford*

Simba Chapter #1, the men, [standing left to right] Michael Holland, Vernal Martin, Joshua Nichols, [seated left to right] Charles Ransom, Rashid Shahid, Donald Walker.

The first Simba Chapter.

The first Simba Instructor Class.

Simba leaders, Keith Ragsdale and Ernest Johnson recruiting volunteers for Simba.
Credit: Steve Faustina

A potential
volunteer reads
over the Simba
Constitution.
*Credit: Steve
Faustina*

Simba leader, Ernest
Johnson answers
questions about
Simba during a
recruitment drive.
Credit: Steve Faustina

Simba boys Markel Abrams, Robert Johnson (below) and Kenny
Dollar (above) enjoy a Simba excursion, learning to sail on Simba supporter
Carl Lynn's 42-foot yacht.

Markel Abrams was not exactly camera shy during this Simba organized sail in the Bay.

Simba men and boys camping at the Police Activities League camping facilities in the east Oakland hills.

Robert Johnson on a movie set starring in a Drug Free America commercial.
Credit: Cindy Fluitt

Roland congratulates Robert Johnson at his sixth-grade graduation. (insert) Robert Johnson with his mother Teena [right] and his grandmother Helen Scott [left], at his sixth-grade graduation.
Credit: Johnson Collection

Keith and Chris at the playground with some of their Chapter's boys.

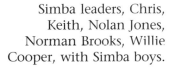

Simba Leaders Keith Ragsdale [left] and Christopher Billups [right].

Simba leaders, Chris, Keith, Nolan Jones, Norman Brooks, Willie Cooper, with Simba boys.

Roland and Alyce proudly oversee a "love" exercise during a Simba leadership seminar. *Credit: Steve Faustina*

Willie Cooper (left) and Michael Holland congratulate Linda Walls at her graduation. *Credit: Steve Faustina*

[left to right] Anthony Harris, Cheo Tyehimba, Karen Moore, and Barbara Staten at final circle graduation. *Credit: Steve Faustina*

Simba leader Cassandra Baines with her sons, who congratulate her upon her graduation, at a Simba training seminar. *Credit: Steve Faustina*

Simba leader Naponisha Sivad.
Credit: Steve Faustina

Simba leader
Nicole Billups.
Credit: Steve Faustina

Simba leader
Michell Shields.
Credit: Steve Faustina

The first Simba Women's Chapter [left to right] Naponisha Sivad, Della Smith, Michell Shields, Nicole Billups, Linda Walls, Karen Moore, Felisha Spiney, Cassandra Baines, Barbara Staten, Cheryl Carswell, Ralondra Ragsdale, Barbara Brooks.
Credit: Steve Faustina

Simba founders Roland and Alyce Gilbert.

Simba's Board of Directors. *Credit: Joel Lewis*

Some of Simba leaders and boys at Lake Merit, Oakland. *Credit: Joel Lewis*

down the street. By her expression, I could tell I was not the person she was expecting.

"Hello Roland. What are you doing over here?" she said.

"Hi Teena! How are you?"

"Fine."

She got up and started up the steps towards her door.

I followed her.

"I just wanted to check on you. It's been awhile, and I was concerned." I said.

"Oh Roland! I'm fine," she insisted.

"Can I come in a minute?" I asked.

"Well, I kinda was expecting company, I have to..."

"I won't stay long."

As I entered the house, I noticed a white piece of paper stapled on the door. It read:

As of July 1, 1989 this mortgaged property is hereby foreclosed. Occupants shall be instructed to vacate premises by said date.

"What's this?" I said.

"Well, you might as well know, I'm outta here. I've lost everything—the house too. But I'm going to kick it here until the new owners move in," she said very nonchalantly.

"Let's go sit down, I want you to tell me what happened," I said.

Inside, there was drug paraphernalia on the coffee table and except for a small chair in the corner, most of her furniture was gone. I sat in the chair, she plopped on the floor. She wouldn't look at me.

"It's OK Teena, I'm not here to judge, I'm here to help. I've been where you are and I know..."

"Oh Roland, I was doing great, you know that. I guess I started to think I was completely over it. You know, that I could smoke just a little bit again. And at first I was fine. Then I started feeling sorry for myself. I was working every day and living from check to check and I wasn't enjoying life. It seemed like all of the people who weren't working were having all of the fun, you know what I mean, like they had it easy. So I thought what the hell, I might as well do it too. So I started missing days at work. I'd call in sick, and pretty soon, weeks went by before I'd go in."

"They finally fired you?"

"Yep. They brought me before a panel review board and told me I was being let go for lack of attendance. After I lost my job, everything else just went to hell. I sent the kids to stay with my mom and I don't know... I guess I just got sick and tired of it all, so I started smoking again. There's a crack house across the street and down the street, so it's easy to get the drugs."

"Did you smoke today?" I said.

"Today? Shit, every day. Before you got here, I was expecting someone to drop me off a package," she said.

"How do you pay for it?" I said.

"Well I don't have much left, but I've been selling stuff. Clothes, furniture, my refrigerator, appliances, everything..."

I looked at her and I could tell she was at the "fuck it" stage, probably the most dangerous stage of the crack addict's descent to "the bottom." And she was days, maybe only hours, from reaching her bottom. I eyed the glass pipe on the table. It looked all too familiar. I'd been clean for about two years, but it was even a temptation for me. I knew I had to get out, quick. I tried to get her to clean up and come with me.

"Look Teena. Why don't you come over to my place and we'll figure all this out together," I said.

"No, no, no. I can't. I told you I'm expecting company. You go on, I'll call you later," she said.

"But Teena, look, there's a better way, you don't have to choose this.

"LOOK ROLAND, I don't have time for you. OK? I know you've helped me in the past, but if you want to really help me now, just leave, OK!?" she said.

I knew if I stayed much longer, we'd wind up in a big argument, and I didn't want that. I also knew that if I stayed much longer, her so-called friends would arrive with a fresh supply of coke and I didn't need that temptation. I wasn't about to make myself a victim trying to help her. When an addict is plummeting to the bottom, there really isn't anything you can do. The desperation in Teena's eyes told me she was quickly on her way and nothing I could say or do would change that.

"Alright Teena. But promise me you'll call me in the morning."

"I promise. See ya!" she said as she flung open the door.

As I walked down the steps to my car, I noticed two women and a young brother coming up the sidewalk. They whisked past me and headed up the steps to Teena's house. She opened the door and they walked right in. Before she closed the door she glanced in my direction—I'll never forget the look on her face: hopeless hope filled her eyes and trickled down onto her face until all that was left was bitter smirk.

She slammed the door and was gone.

I got in my car and went home.

"OK y'all, it's ON!" said Teena.

"What is this shit, it ain't even rocked-up yet! Y'all know I don't snort! Alright, who's gonna cook!" she continued.

Some time later when everything was ready, they sat down on the floor in Teena's living room, to light up.

Then there was a knock on the door.

It was "Slow," a guy from down the street. Slow was a heroin user. He had lived in East Oakland all his life and for as long as anybody could remember, people called him "Slow." Although no one really knew why, because he wasn't slow, especially when it came to hustling.

"Yo Teena, I got some new tennis shoes here. I'll sell them to you," he said.

"I don't need any shoes, Slow."

"Wait! I don't want money, I'll sell 'em to you for a dub," he said.

Teena let him come in to show the shoes to the others, but no one wanted them and he was disappointed.

"OK, if that's the way y'all gonna be," he said as he walked out.

An hour later there was a knock at the door.

"Will you get that," Teena said.

"It's Slow, he wants to come in," said the brother at the door.

"Let him in," Teena said.

Slow walked through the smoke-filled, dimly lit room, bumping into things and feeling his way around until, finally, he was in front of the group. His large shadow flickered off the back wall as Teena and the others worked to keep their pipes lit. He still had the shoes, but he wasn't trying to sell them anymore. Without saying a word, he laid the shoes down and sat in the chair in the corner. Then someone passed him a small rock and a pipe. He took it, smiled, and quickly joined them on the floor.

After a few minutes, he picked up his pipe and got ready to smoke, but the rock was gone. Almost immediately, Slow began crawling on his hands and knees, frantically looking for the rock.

"What happened to my shit? What happened to my shit?!!" he said.

He stood up and walked over to Teena.

"Teena!! What happened to my shit?" he said standing directly over her.

Teena didn't hear him. He leaned over and slapped her hard across the face. The pipe Teena was holding flew through the air and crashed into the wall.

"Shut up!" Slow shouted. "Don't say a motherfucking thing, bitch!" he continued.

Everyone stopped smoking, no one moved.

Slow pulled out a jagged buck knife and grabbed Teena by the arm and yanked her up. He put the knife up to her throat.

"EVERYBODY GET THE FUCK OUT," Slow shouted. "Now! or I'll cut her throat and if you don't think I'll do it just watch!" he said.

The knife pressed cold against Teena's throat. Her eyes widened with fear as she watched her "friends" run out the door.

"It's all your fault. You told them not to buy the shoes from me," Slow shouted.

"Slow, I told them about your shoes and no one wanted them," Teena said nervously.

"Shut up!" Slow said as he dragged her towards the door.

Slow swung open the door and dragged Teena outside. It was past 3 a.m. and the night was dead—the streets empty. Holding Teena by the arm with one hand and holding the knife at her throat with the other, Slow dragged her down the steps and onto the street. But instead of dragging her down Bancroft Avenue, which is a main street, he turned and forced her down the alley next to her house, until they came to a gate leading into her neighbor's backyard.

"Get in there!" Slow whispered.

Slow dragged Teena from backyard to back yard. Every time she tried to talk to him, he squeezed her arm tighter and threatened her with the knife. He dragged her through six different backyards until they finally arrived at his girlfriend's backyard, two blocks away.

Holding Teena against the side of the house, Slow pulled out a small gun.

"I want to shoot you," he whispered. "But I really like you... RUN, so I can shoot you. *Please* run so I can shoot you!" he said.

Teena was frozen. She knew if she moved or jerked away, he'd slash her with the knife. If she ran, he was crazy enough to shoot her in the back. She kept thinking this isn't happening to me. This can't be happening. I haven't talked with my family in weeks and I'm about to die over a little white rock, in a part of town where nobody, including the police, gives a fuck.

She thought of her family and how they'd react to her death. She thought about her mother and the day she had come bursting into her house to "save" her from crack. On that day, Teena had been sitting with a friend in her room when all of a sudden, her bedroom door burst open and her mother walked in.

"I'm here to reclaim my daughter! In the name of Jesus, get out of this house!" she shouted, pointing her finger at the man sitting on Teena's bed.

"What are you talking about?" Teena shouted. "Save me? We ain't smoking and I don't need to be saved by you. I do what I want to do and you ain't running my life no more, mama."

But now, as she felt Slow's tight grip slowly begin to release on her limp arm, she wished there was someone, anyone, who could save her.

"No, I'm not going to run."

"Why?! Just run! *Pleeaase!.*"

Teena closed her eyes and didn't move and inch.

"I'll shoot yo ass, then!"

He cocked the gun and pointed it at her head.

He squeezed the trigger.

Click.

"Naw, there's a couple bullets in this muthafucka. I know that! I'll just try it again," Slow whispered.

"Wait, I'll run! Slow, stop it, I'll run! I'll run!" Teena pleaded.

Then there was a loud knock at the front door.

Immediately, Slow dropped the gun and put the knife back up to Teena's throat. He dragged her around to the front of the house to see who it was.

Nessie, his girlfriend's friend, was knocking on the door. She was a heroin user too and she looked desperate.

Dragging Teena, Slow ran and grabbed Nessie. She kicked and screamed.

"Shhh! Shut up Nessie! Come here! Hold still!" he said.

"Slow, is that you? What are doing? Get off me! Let me go! What is this! HELP!" she screamed.

Nessie fought wildly and Teena struggled to get away. Amid the flurry, Slow slashed through the darkness and stabbed Nessie in the thigh.

She let out a piercing scream and reached for her leg.

Then someone opened the front door.

It was Slow's girlfriend.

"Who's out there?"

She flicked the porch light on.

"Slow, what are you doing to them?! Are you crazy? Let them go!" she said.

"Go back in the house. Please! And don't call the police," Slow hissed.

"I won't call, just let them go!" she said.

"Get in the house!" Slow screamed.

She went back in and closed the door.

Slow held Teena against the wall with one hand and had Nessie, who was hunched over in pain, grabbing her bloody leg, by her arm. He didn't know what to do next. Sweat dripped from his face and he was breathing heavily.

"See whatchu went and did, Nessie? You weren't supposed to be in this! All I wanted to do was sell my shoes for a dub so I could sell it to Marty over on Foothill. He promised me some crack, now I ain't got shit!" he said frantically.

"I gotta get my shit! and if I have to kill both of you to do it, I will!" he said.

Just then, Nessie's boyfriend appeared at the entrance to the backyard, hiding a baseball bat behind his back.

"Hey man, why don't you just let them go. I'm not going to do anything to you, just let them go," he said.

"Hey Brian, this ain't for you, man. Ain't nobody bothering you. Stay back!" Slow said as he backed up.

All of a sudden, Brian rushed Slow like a madman, swinging the bat violently and hollering, "Let 'em go! Let 'em go!"

Slow immediately let go of the girls and picked up the gun. He fired and missed. Teena and Nessie took off up the street. Brian swung the bat and hit Slow in the hands. The gun went flying. Then he swung again—and again—and again—by the time the police arrived, everybody was gone and Slow, bloody and beaten, had to be carried off to Highland Hospital.

Teena ran all the way home and locked her door. She threw away all of the crack paraphernalia that was still in the house. She sat down on her bed, and began to cry. It was 5 a.m. and the sun was coming up. She picked up the phone and dialed.

"Hello?" I answered.

"Roland, it's Teena" she said.

"Teena...oh what's the problem? What time is it? What's wrong?" I said.

She didn't say anything.

"Have you been using?" I said.

"Yes" she said.

"Oh Teena... OK. This is what I want you to do. Get up and take a bath. Change your sheets. Throw anything that has the smell on it away. Then go to sleep, get some rest. I'll come over this afternoon and we'll talk. OK?"

There was no response.

"Teena! Teena! Did you hear me!" I said.

"Yes Roland, I'll do it. You're right. I'll do it."

After her house was sold, Teena joined her children and moved into her mother's three-bedroom apartment by Lake Merritt. She stopped smoking crack, but it continued to be a day-to-day struggle for her. In fact, I know she's had a few relapses. Over the months to come, despite my on-again off-again contact with Teena, I managed to develop a good relationship with her son, Robert. We still went to church regularly, and when Simba first opened its doors, Robert was the first boy to join. His father was completely out of his life. In fact, even today, Robert doesn't know where his father is, or even if he is alive or dead. Robert was at serious risk of becoming another victim of the ghetto. Teena's other two children, Monita and Jamila, were equally "at-risk." Although they had now moved in with their grandmother on the other side of town, the family pain, bitterness, and dysfunction was apparent. Even the beautiful view of Lake Merritt couldn't erase that.

In many ways, the Johnsons were the typical African American family in the nineties—the father absent, and the mother struggling to support her children with a menial, low-paying job that offers no stability. Drugs and emotional, spiritual, and physical violence flowed like blood through the family, generation after generation. There's a popular theory today in the African American community. It says: *All we have to do is go back to the old way we did things*. Many of our churches talk about that Good 'Ole Time Religion and how we need to return to it. Well, let's take a closer look at this. Most of our current thinking patterns came from that 'Ole Time Religion, which we practiced while working from "can't see in the morning 'til can't see at night" on somebody's plantation. But as illogical as this thinking is, it persists today and is usually voiced by the older generation. And since so many of our children are being raised by their grandmothers, the "old school" spare-the-rod-spoil-the-child psychology continues to shatter the esteem of our black boys.

And so it was with the Johnson family.

When Robert turned twelve, he started his year-long Simba Rites-of-Passage manhood training. A few months into his training, he began to question his mother when she disciplined him. During his training, Robert learned about keeping his agreements and how to positively resolve conflicts. With each step in the passage, Robert was learning self-control principles that his family was completely unfamiliar with. So now, when family arguments came up, the usual "because I said so" reply offered by his mother or grandmother no longer resolved the issue. Robert wanted explanations, but the women authority figures in his life didn't think he needed one. "Because I said so" had always been enough for them, and he'd have to learn to accept it. They saw his new confidence as a threat.

I explained to his mother that Robert was learning how to "be on purpose" in every area of his life, and that it might require him to question authority. After a few meetings, she agreed not to strike him anymore. And that was tough for her.

As a single parent, hitting was the fastest way for her to get the behavior she wanted. And after all, she was only doing what she'd learned from her parents—that children must be controlled. Eventually, I got her to understand the inherent danger in that philosophy and its long-range detrimental effects. I explained that we must learn to *guide* our children, not control them.

One morning after church, while I was driving Robert home, he began to tell me about one of his latest encounters with his grandmother: He had come home from school and she was scolding him for not making up his bed.

"When they made the Johnsons, they really messed up," she said.

"You can say that all you want but that don't make it true," said Robert.

"What did you say?" she said.

"I said, just because you say it, doesn't make you right."

She shook her finger at him.

"Oh, boy, I just can't wait until y'all move out. All y'all too smart for me! Humph! That's right! Y'all was supposed to move out in March, but I gave your stupid mama a chance."

"Why you want us to move?"

"Well... look at this room! This isn't how I keep my house! When y'all used to live on 65th Avenue in East Oakland, y'all treated your house anyway you wanted. But this is my house and I want y'all to treat my house different! And you ain't been doing it. I can't wait until y'all move in August! And I know your momma ain't even looking for a house. I don't know why she keeps coming home saying she looked when she really didn't. I don't like this and I'm tired of putting up with your momma!" she said.

"Well tell her, don't tell me!" said Robert.

"Oh, I do tell your mom. I want y'all to move. I want your mom to get you and your sister out of here!" she said.

"And don't just yell at her so everybody in the house can hear you. She ain't gonna listen to you when you do that."

"Well, I don't think it matters."

"Grandma, you always look at the bad stuff we do. Why don't you see our *greatness* grandma?" said Robert.

"Greatness!? Y'all ain't got no greatness and I ain't got no greatness. If I don't have no greatness, then y'all ain't got none," she snapped.

"You don't have no greatness, grandma?"

"No"

"I know some greatness you have," said Robert.

"Well that's just your definition. We must have different definitions," she said.

"OK, but how can we get in agreement?"

"*Agreement*? What? I ain't in no agreement!" she said.

"I mean, you're mad at everybody because of mom. But how can *we* get in agreement so that me and you can have a better relationship?"

"I don't want to make no agreement, Robert. I just don't want to."

"Fine. OK Grandma. I guess you're just a "won't know," and you have to be right, and you'll never know."

"That's right," she said.

"Fine. Then I don't want to communicate with you anymore. I'm going to listen and do what you say, but when it comes to just talking, I don't think I want to do it, because you're really not open!"

"Fine!" she said as she walked in the bathroom.

There was a long silence and I could tell that Robert was still contemplating his actions, wondering if he'd handled the conflict with his grandmother correctly.

"We stopped talking for a couple of days after that. Roland... when I use what I've learned in Simba with my family, it seems like it only makes them madder at me. I guess she's just acting the way her mother and father raised her to act. I just got to learn how to live with it and not be a victim," said Robert.

"Robert, your analysis is right on target! I'm proud of the way you handled that situation, but remember, its *never* the other person, regardless of the negative energy or attitude they give you, *you* must always maintain self-control."

"I'm trying, but it's hard sometimes."

"I know. Listen, Robert when dealing with your family, it's not as simple as choosing to 'not communicate' with them. You have to learn to accept them as they are. Your grandmother has something to offer you and there's a reason she's in your life right now, and there's a reason that you are in conflict with her. Be thankful for it, because it's a great opportunity for you to discover your stuff and to learn to deal with your stuff," I said.

"OK Roland, I'll try harder."

"That's great Robert! I'm proud of you."

Chapter 8

Three Generations
of African American Thought

Grandmother: Helen Scott Johnson, 59, Retired.

I was born November 6, 1933 in Pensicana, Texas. It sits on the border of Texas and Arkansas. I am an only child. I have an uncle who lives on 44th street in Oakland, and the rest of my relatives are in Houston. I moved to California with my parents at the age of four. My mother and father were divorced when I was fourteen. I started school here in Oakland on 62nd and San Pablo at Golden Gate school and I went all the way through and graduated from there in 1947. Then I went to Oakland Tech, and graduated from there in 1950 and I got married in 1950. I had three children, one son and two daughters. I met my husband through my mother. After she and my father divorced, I was visiting with her at a party and I met my husband there. He was quite a bit older than me, seventeen years. At the party, I guess I was being what they call a "show off," you know, I was showing the older women, "Hey, you know whatever I want, I get, so I got "caught" by him.

After twelve years, we finally divorced. I don't believe in people staying together and not getting along and we weren't. There was a lot of turmoil so we decided together—I initiated it but we decided together—that this was probably the best thing to do. He was a good father, but they thought he was mean because of our differences. He came from what people called the "old school." His grandparents raised him and he believed and thought that everybody should be raised a certain way—in other words—"don't spare the rod," and I felt he used it a little too much, so we had difficulty about that. I believe kids should be disciplined. They should be spanked, whipped, whatever word you want to use, but within reason. I think kids should have chores, curfews—something to do after school so they are not hanging around. They should be disciplined so that any grown-up could tell a child that you're doing something wrong and you show respect. We don't have that now and my kids had it and I had it. When I was raised up you didn't curse, you didn't do a lot of things in front of older people.

It's different now. Oh, I think it's outrageous nowadays because kids have no respect for anybody. Now with the drug situation, there are a lot of grandparents raising kids. "He won't wear this! She won't wear this! I have to buy him something else..." they say. What do you mean he won't? Why won't he?

The parent has let the child take over and I don't really know where it all started. I guess it started with people thinking that this is the way I show my child that I love him. But that's not right. They need discipline. I believe kids need a lot of discipline regardless. I don't think they have to have a father in the house to have discipline, it all depends on how you start out with them. You can't start out telling them "I don't care if you do such and such" and then later try to put your foot down. It's too late. You have to have a guideline that you start out with and hold to it.

In 1964, I went and got a real estate license and worked in that business up until, I guess '82 or '83. I didn't work regularly at it because it was not as profitable as one thinks. When I went into it, it was not as profitable because as blacks, we didn't have the properties to offer, people didn't have the money to buy them, and we had sections where blacks couldn't move. I took other jobs like waitressing, which I found myself doing more and more in order to have money.

When Robert was considering joining Simba, he came in and sat down and we talked. At first I didn't agree upon it. I asked what does *Simba* mean and so forth and they explained to me that it was an African idea or what have you, and I didn't first agree on Robert joining it for the simple reason that I don't particularly care for Africans because they don't care for me. Usually they give you the impression that they are better than American blacks. I've talked to them and I knew some that went to the university, I've met some in Reno, and then there are quite a few here on Grand Avenue. And they totally ignore you and for that reason I didn't think much of it [SIMBA] and I didn't care for it.

I used to work in a restaurant called John Singers down in West Oakland. There used to be a lot of African students that would come in. It was open 24 hours a day. And after two o'clock, and everything was closed up, most of them came to pick up food and that was my first experience with dealing with African people. I worked as a cook and a waitress. As an American, if you could pronounce their name or say something intelligent they looked at you funny and thought—hey, you can read my name. Also, twice, it happened on the bus when I had no other choice but to sit next to this African man because that was the only seat, and he and I talked all the way back. He started telling me about American black people. He was like—you people are so stupid—you let these white people do this and do that—and I said, "Hold it, just one minute. I'm not the one that sold my brother for a trinket, and I'm not the one who let the white man take my diamond mines, so don't give me that shit 'cause I don't want to hear it." Oh we talked all the way, and before he got off the bus he said, "I understand what you saying."

We didn't argue, but I explained to him how I felt and how I saw things with the native Africans as compared to me—and how I didn't bring myself over here and I didn't sell my brother to people. So he understood a little better about us. Right here, they have businesses up and down the street and they act like they really don't care if you come in or not. They'll look at you like you have dirt on you. And they are all that way. I don't find white people to be like that as much as they are. The Africans don't seem to give you any respect. I know what I see. I see them not caring about me, so I don't care about them, and I'm that way about anybody.

So me and Robert talked about Simba and he explained that it is not really an African thing all together, but its all about men helping boys that need help to become better young men. Simba has helped Robert a lot because Robert is like most of the children today—they don't want discipline, they don't want to accept the word "no." First of all, especially our black men need to accept that word because if you don't accept the word no, then you get in trouble. No means No—to rape, to stealing, to anything. No. If you understand the word no, you might not like it, but you can accept it, instead of rolling your eyes and asking why and complaining. I'm not talking about saying no to a positive idea. I'm not speaking about saying no to something that educates or helps the child. I'm talking about the no you say when a child says he wants to go play 'stead of doing his chores, or every time a child wants to buy this or that, or every time a child says can he go around the corner. He has to learn how to accept "no," because if he can't accept it from his parents then he can't accept it from anybody else. And then you're in trouble. That's a trouble thing, to not to learn to accept "no" in the outside world.

My relationship with Robert is fine. Before Simba, Robert wouldn't dare talk back to me or roll his eyes. But now at the age of fourteen, when there's something he don't like, he's like a little baddy rooster, he "expresses" himself. Expressing himself is OK to a certain point, but I think sometimes he goes a little beyond that. Most kids go beyond it because its the times. And the parents, like in his case, people Teena's age, some of 'em think that kids are supposed to "express" themselves. But there's a way of doing everything. I mean there's a certain respect that children should give to adults.

Robert's future can be good, provided he wants to be something, and depending on how bad he wants to be it. Because, regardless of what people say, if you want to do something, you'll do it. It's just that simple.

And Robert is kind of a go-getter, so he will do it, and depending on what it is, more than likely, he will have my support. I'm not speaking of financial support, but I can encourage him. If I know anything about what he's trying to do, I will give him my input. But things have changed a lot since I was going to school, and there are some things I just can't help him with. Right now our relationship is kind of stormy because he thinks I'm mean. I try to explain things to him and he'll say "I understand." Then, two days later, he'll come up with something else similar to what I had just explained to him, and he'll go off. So either he didn't really understand after all or he thinks he knows. That's one problem I find with Robert, you try to tell him something and he says "Oh, I know." But he don't know. And he resents me, a lot. And I know it, but its just one of those things. I feel that I'm being fair with him. What I be fussing at him or telling him about is something to help him not just today, but further down the road, and I explain that to him.

Mother: Teena Johnson, 39, Waitress.

After I graduated from Piedmont High School, I went to Alameda College but I only lasted for a year. I knew I was soon going to get married. I was in love and I didn't think I needed to stay in school. Then I got pregnant on purpose. I'd been taking birth control. We were already engaged and we planned to get married, but he didn't want me to get pregnant. I missed a day taking my pills and he found out. So I took a whole bunch of pills to compensate. And I got sick. Then I just let my body readjust without taking the pills. He was always so insistent that I don't get pregnant and I was pissed. So I thought that I would just let myself get pregnant, to spite him. I know it sounds crazy. I was twenty when I got pregnant and I was married by early 1975.

We stayed together for ten years. We divorced because he was an insatiable gambler. He loved horse races. He followed them around the state.

He did work, that was not a problem. He was a shoe repairer, and I worked at the post office. We both made good money. We had a house in 1977 on 65th and Bancroft. It was a two-bedroom house. We converted it and added another room to it. The rent went up and the problems started. He was gambling our money away.

Then I got sick and I had to go into the hospital. I was working at the post office and I didn't have any sick leave. So after my surgery, when I was home recuperating, I didn't have any money coming in, but at least I knew I had a job when I got back. When I got home from the hospital, I noticed a lot of unpaid bills. PGE was going to cut us off and my daughter had been sent home because her bills hadn't been paid at the school—my kids were going to private schools. My husband knew he was supposed to pay the bills while I was in the hospital, but he didn't. After that, I knew I was through. That was in 1981. I divorced him, and I got the house and the kids. He was supposed to be able to visit whenever he wanted, though he never visited them often. The divorce was final in 1982.

About two years later, I met this guy and we started going out. Then we were supposed to be getting married. We set the date for January 1984. We had sent out invitations and made all of the plans. One day he was supposed to pick me up after work and he never showed up. I called and he wasn't at home, I called his parents and no one had seen him. I questioned him, and he told me he was out with his ex-girlfriend. On the day after Christmas, he told me he was having second thoughts. He was at my house and he was really procrastinating on last minute details for the wedding. I could just sense that he did not want to get married. We discussed it, and he finally told me that he didn't want to get married. He decided to go back to his ex-girlfriend. He said that he wanted to continue to see his ex-girlfriend. All the invitations were out, so I had to send out cancellation letters to all those people. I was very calm.

He had been with his ex-girlfriend for years. They had one of those relationships where they would break up and then get back together and then break up and get back together. I realized he was not going to leave this woman. One day he called me and said he wanted to have a meeting. He wanted all three of us to live together. We met and discussed this in detail and we decided to do it. We even set a date. After I got home, I sat down and thought about what had just happened. It was crazy. I called him and told him I couldn't do it. A month later, we stopped seeing each other.

From January until April 1984, I stayed in my room and locked the door. I didn't go to work. I didn't answer the phone. I didn't talk to anybody. I was devastated. Eventually I just realized it was an obsession. It wasn't love. I guess he was just filling a void. I was extremely angry and hurt. I was embarrassed. I felt totally stupid. I had always believed in love—getting married and living happily ever after, a house, two kids, and a car—the whole bit.

When I first moved in with my mother, I used crack at least once a week, if not more. My mother knew. Most times if I went out, I went back to my old stomping grounds, East Oakland, and I'd stay out all night. I was sure that my children knew, but I never talked about it with them. After I'd go to CA meetings, I'd bring home the pamphlets and leave them on the table. So I know they saw them. They never asked me any questions and I never volunteered any information. And I still haven't to this day. My mother knows. We don't get along and we never have. When I started using drugs, it just got worse. She made a statement one time, "Of all three of my children, I never would of expected this from you," she said. It was like I was on this pedestal and I didn't want that. I was always considered the responsible kid. I was the one who got married. All three of my kids were by the same father. We bought a house and I had a good job. So, any time I ever did anything, it was like, "Oh no, not Teena." This is why I never came to anybody in my family and said anything, because I wasn't supposed to have any problems. I'd feel like I'd let everybody down or something. So rather than do that, I just didn't say anything. My family doesn't understand about my struggle with drugs, and I don't feel that I get any support.

At the beginning of my addiction, I went to CA for awhile, and it helped me at first, but after awhile it became cliquish, just like any other group. Those that had been there a long time seemed to get all of the support. Those that were new, like me, were lost. I felt totally isolated. When the meetings are over, everybody gets into these little groups and there you are, just there. I didn't get a sponsor. No one ever came up to me. All of the stories were about drugs. People talked so much about drugs, I'd leave there and want to go get high because it had been put on my mind so much. So I stopped going after about six months.

After awhile it got so bad that I didn't go to work until payday, and then it was only to pick up my check so I could go buy some more crack. It got to the point where I got high everyday. Sometimes I'd be so high I'd be scared to come down. Because whenever I came off a high, there was always this awful jittery feeling. I'd be too scared to go to sleep, because I'd think I wasn't going to wake up. I was pathetic.

Right now I'm struggling. I'm truly struggling. I still have urges daily. I have dreams about drugs. I dream that I'm somewhere and I'm getting high, and I see everything. It be seriously real. When I see someone smoking crack on television, and there are other people in the room who know I've used, I feel guilty. It's like "I know everybody is looking at me." I feel I got to explain... right now I'm not smoking because, ahh... right this minute I'm not smoking because...

Right now I choose not to do it, but it's a daily struggle. I think about drugs everyday. I haven't gotten to the point where I can say I'll never smoke again. The worst thing is, people think they can control it. It's not the same type of addiction, but it's an addiction. To me, it's even worse than Heroin, because you never get enough. People on Heroin, they get their fix that they need to keep from being sick and then they can do without for awhile. You don't get sick from crack. You never get "high" enough. As long as there's a way to get some, you can smoke from morning to midnight. You can smoke yourself to death. People will smoke and drop dead. Before I started smoking, I talked about other people I knew who smoked. They had lost their jobs, their homes and I thought— How could they let that happen? I would never... And now I'm guilty of the same thing.

If someone were to show up right now and they were to tell me they had some, I'd be tempted. When I worked at Denny's, and I knew I had a check coming, I'd take one of the kids with me to go get my check—to make sure. Because with the kids with me, I won't do anything. Sometimes I just have to take extra precautions. My future is up to me. There are lots of things that I can't do because I don't have the skills or the money. I don't even have the money for transportation. The only goal I have right now is to move out of my mother's house.

Simba has helped Robert a lot. Robert has gained more confidence in life itself. Because of all of the things he had going on around him, for Simba to come in, it made a real difference in his life. Robert has become more responsible. He has become more aggressive, in a good and bad way. There have been a couple of times where we have gotten into confrontations and he mentions Simba. And I think, "Oh, this is coming from Simba." But Simba has been something we've needed for a long time. Its emphasis on black boys is important. We talk about all being equal and all this. And to just look at people as people. The reality is life is different for black kids than it is for white kids or Mexican kids. We're all different.

Son: Robert Johnson, 14, Student

I'm the youngest. One of my sisters is sixteen and the other one is eighteen. The sixteen-year-old is Monita Johnson and she goes to Oakland Tech. She likes to baby-sit, so that's how she makes her money and stuff. My other sister is Jamila Johnson and she just turned eighteen. She goes to Cal Berkeley.

When we lived in East Oakland, my father used to come

and visit. And I was happy to see him. I remember whenever he left, I would sit up on this chair that's right behind the window and I'd watch him crossing the street, and I'd just start crying. One day he took me to Golden Gate fields to watch a horse race.

Then on the way back he stopped in West Oakland by San Pablo and he goes into a house. He says, "you stay here."

Then this girl comes out from the house and says "Who are you?" I told her who I was and that I was waiting for my dad. "You want to know what your dad is doing back there?" she said. "He in there doing drugs."

"Naw, naw, I don't believe you."

"Do you want to come in and call your mom?" she said.

"No, no Leave me alone!" I said and I started crying. Then my dad came out and I told him.

"You just have to ignore her, she just likes me."

I didn't know what to believe. He was in there for about thirty minutes.

Another time he called me and said he was going to pick me up and that we were going to spend the whole day together. I waited that Saturday... he didn't call, he never came or nothing. And even after that Saturday, he still didn't call.

The next time I saw him was when I saw him in front of my school. He looked like he wasn't healthy. He looked bad. He was right in front of my school and I stopped and I looked at him and I'm like, that can't be him, he kind of looks like the campus supervisor. Then I realized that it was him, so I walked up to him and said, "We got to talk." He gave me his new address on a card. He told me to write him and he gave me a cherry pie and a twinkie. I ate the twinkie but I kept the pie to remember that I saw him.

Eventually, I wrote him, but I never got anything back. So Roland went to the address to find out what was going on. We thought that maybe he didn't want to see me. Roland got there and found out the address was to a shoe store. And we found out that this was where he had worked, but didn't work there anymore. So we called his sister's number, and she says she hadn't seen him either. I haven't seen him or talked to him since that day—and that was several years ago. I don't know where my father is. Now I don't know if he's dead or what.

He never did what he said he was going to do. I don't like him that much, not like I used to. I drew my line, but I keep forgiving him. I give him too many chances and he keeps hurting me, but I don't want to let him keep hurting me.

If I see him again, I'll talk to him, but I won't want to communicate with him. I don't want to go nowhere with him anymore. Besides, he's probably forgot all about me, and I think he's on drugs now.

I think maybe his parents did the same thing to him. He has his intentions, but he's letting his programs run for him. He doesn't choose the program. He doesn't keep his agreements, because that's all he knows how to do. He can change at any time. Everyone else can tell him how to change, but he is the only one that can change his habits. I'm not going to hate him and I'm not going to beat myself up the rest of my life because of what he does. I just don't want to be his friend anymore. If he decides that one day, after he gets a good job, he's just going to be able to come to me and all of a sudden be in my life, it's not going to work like that. It's not that easy. He's got to earn my respect.

There are a lot of homes now with just the mother. And the children are mostly males. That's why they have Simba. Like me for instance, all I have is women in my house. So where am I going to get all the stuff that I need to know about being a man?

Roland has helped me. He is like another father to me. He's like a big role model. I think he's intelligent and creative. He always backs up what he says and he knows what he's talking about. He's very open and honest. If he's mad at me or my mom, he's not afraid to let us know. I like that my mom doesn't object to Roland. She trusts him. I thought she would get mad because I spend a lot of time with Roland. When he goes away, a lot of people are going to be shocked and hurt, but he says he's going to live to be 150!

Before Simba, I used be out on the street from 9:00 to 9:00 every day—school in the mornings and then after school at three o'clock—I'd be out. Simba is about African American men coming and helping African American boys to grow up and become African American men who will continue to help. If I needed some help, they've always been there. Simba has helped me with my anger programs. A program is a habitual way of thinking, and so Simba has been a support to me in helping me control my anger and Simba has helped me in being more open. I've learned not to be afraid to tell someone exactly how I feel. Simba has taught me what my issues are: profanity, anger, violence (but not so much), self-worth, and trust. I don't trust people because of what's happened in the past.

I have big plans for my future. First I want to graduate from high school. Then hopefully I'll get a scholarship to UC Berkeley. I'm going to major in mathematics and get a Ph.D. Then I'm going to run for governor and be governor for maybe one or two terms. Then I'm going to have my own business in some kind of corporation in sales or marketing. Then, after that, I'm going to sell the company and become President of the United States. I'm going to repaint the White House. It'll be black, white, yellow, brown, and red. It's going to be the "People's House." When my term is over as president, I'll go back into business. I'm going to have a wife and then have a boy and girl, and have a big house, two cars, and lots of money. I want to be at least a millionaire. After that, I would go back to teaching as a professor at a university. And, of course, I'll be working with Simba also. That's pretty much how I see myself living. Living large.

We don't know about ourselves and our ancestors... our heroes. Heroes like Marcus Garvey, Martin Luther King Jr., and Harriet Tubman. The only time we learn about our heroes is in February—at least at school, and then it's only at an assembly, and since we only have assemblies once a week, that's only four days a year! But we African Americans need to learn more about our history everyday. We don't know the truth. The Afrocentric point of view. We know everything that the white man believes. From history, we should learn that the white man's way is not really the way to get what we want.

We may have been born and raised in a black neighborhood, but what we were taught was what the white man believed— all of the different "programs," and the Eurocentric point of view. So what the Ghetto Solution is, is Simba. Simba teaches the Afrocentric world view and how to get what we want. After we learn it, we apply it to our lives. Then, the boys that are learning now will teach the next generation, and they will teach the next, and so on. Simba never stops.

Robert's Journal

I developed a specialized rites-of-passage program for all of the boys in Simba, Inc. It consists of twelve levels of development that the boy must complete before he is initiated into manhood. Throughout each step, the boy develops a greater sense of self through spiritual, cultural, psychological, emotional, and intellectual analysis. He also develops values based on the *Nguzo Saba* or "Seven Principles of Blackness" developed by Dr. Maulana Karenga. They are: *Umoja* (Unity); *Kujichagulia* (Self-Determination); *Ujima* (Collective Work & Responsibility); *Ujamaa* (Cooperative Economics); *Nia* (Purpose); *Kuumba* (Creativity); and *Imani* (Faith).

Through each step, the boy is assigned several external activities such as: community service projects, attending worship service regularly, researching and making presentations on African and African American topics, developing business and career skills, learning positive affirmations, and many, many more. But the most important skill the boy learns is *self-analysis*. This is above all else. His greatest challenge is the development of his "I AM." Throughout the passage the boy keeps a journal and documents his innermost thoughts on his journey. During Robert's passage, he had to write in his journal on several topics. The following are excerpts from his entries, listed chronologically:

Robert at Twelve:

What I'm Afraid of is...

To walk alone at night in public, to go down the street to KFC [Kentucky Fried Chicken] because somebody got shot there, to go to a funeral, to go over by Acorn [projects], to go by the Cypress Structure because it reminds me of the earthquake, to go to West Oakland. I'm afraid of dying and for my family to die.

The African American Man is...

A beast, a liar, a smart man, another Martin Luther King, Jr., another Malcolm X, another Frederick Douglas, a leader, a boxer, a football player, a baseball player, a basketball player, a skinny man, a medium man, a fat man, a short man, a tall man, a man you can trust, a man you can depend on, a man you can love.

What I want for me is...

All the arcade toys and video games, love, not hate, of course peace, a fun, exciting life, a long life, to come back alive, you know, reincarnation, for everyone to love me, to love the one and only God and Jesus and Lucifer, but only so that he'll turn back to good and won't nobody have to think of the word hell. And last but not least, to always have my mommy.

What I'm angry about...

On school nights I have to go to bed too early. That my grandma is always cussing in front of me, and its not always for a good reason. But I guess it's not always her fault that I can't have my own TV or have an allowance. But I'm mostly angry that I can't have my dad.

What I've learned about me...

I have a greatness deep inside me and I deserve what I want. That I am a winner, that I am worthy, that I am proud of who I am and can't no one change that. I have the ability to believe and have trust in myself. That I am smart, creative, talented, and a good reader, a good teacher, a good human being, and a good sports player.

How I feel about my grandmother...

Sometimes bad, sometimes happy, sometimes I feel real mad, and sometimes I feel that she is nice. Sometimes I get real mad at her because she curses a lot. She curses the most in the house, too. Sometimes I feel as though she should just leave my life, yeah, I know that's pretty heavy. Sometimes I feel sorry for her. Sometimes I think she's mean. I know that I say that I hate her, but I don't really mean it.

How I feel about my environment is...

My environment can be better and I believe that my environment is trying to be the best that it can be. Besides, why would anyone hate their environment when all they're saying is "I hate myself." You see it's a rumor going around saying whites are better than blacks, but all you have to know is that you are human no matter what. If you're black, white, oriental, Cambodian, etc. that doesn't matter see, you are what you are, don't change yourself into something else. You can get anything done on the outside, but remember you can't change the inside because you are what you are. I believe that, do you?

How I feel about Simba...

I feel as though I should owe them something. Why? Because I don't deserve what they're giving me until I realize that I am somebody. Simba is like another school that I get to go to. I'm not going to lie, there are some Simba Leaders that I do sometimes get mad at, but notice I always end up forgiving them—that's where love comes in.

How I feel about my father

I feel disappointed. I feel angry that my dad never came that Saturday that he was supposed to come. The big thing is that he hasn't even called. I feel as if he didn't care, but I will always love him, always remember him, always forgive him, always need him. You see my dad is much more than my dad, he's my Mr. Number One.

Robert at Thirteen:

What I'm afraid of...

I am afraid that all African Americans won't get the chance to find out who they really are because too many African Americans think low of themselves. So many are standing on the streets, and so many say we can't never do anything. Well, there isn't such a word as "can't." You always have a choice. And for this situation the choices are to keep doing drugs, lying on the street, murdering people, etc. or we can choose to become SOMEBODY. To get up and reach out. Be proud of who you are, say I am somebody, I am somebody, I am somebody!

Why I don't do what I say I'll do...

Because sometimes I do too many things at the same time. I do know that I sometimes break promises and just my word. That makes it seem like I don't care what I say. Actually, there are no excuses, besides me just not being "on purpose."

What I want most in life is...

I mostly want my dad back. I know I keep bringing this

subject up, but its very important to me and I'm going to keep bringing it up from time to time. And Roland, I hope you understand. You're like a father to me, but I can't call you "dad" because it's only one person that can be a dad for me, and he is Robert Paul Johnson, my dad.

Why I resent my Grandma...
Because I'm being a victim, I'm letting programs run for me. Programs like "gotta be right." I'm in resentment with what she does. Such things as when I come home almost every night and arguing, not asking no questions, and assuming things, making an ass out of me and her. I try to ignore, I sometimes cut her off, I talk back, I try to get the last word, but that's how I resist the problem. But then no one wins, I'm right but I don't get what I want. It's time to solve the problem. To forgive and let go, 'cause that's what I want.

What is a victim...
The difference between being a victim and a winner. Being a victim is being controlled by someone else. That certainly does not make you a winner. A victim is being defined, named, created, and spoken for by others.

What Simba means to me...
Well, to me Simba means a lot. It first of all means young lion in Swahilli, but the group Simba means BLACK. And black means a lot—African American. Simba has helped me a lot. I have learned how to set goals and also to achieve them. Also to make sure my goals are SMART. SMART stands for specific, measurable, attainable, risk, and time. I've learned how to make and say affirmations. I know now how to visualize and think.

Chapter 9

Lifework

The area in downtown Oakland known as Jack London Square is one of Oakland's most historic landmarks. It's situated south of the port of Oakland, on the water, and surrounded by a complex of mediocre hotels, novelty shops, restaurants, and burgeoning businesses. Like many other areas downtown, the waterfront has been in constant transition, although for some reason the area has never gained the kind of national popularity, commerce, and widespread development that has graced another historic waterfront just across the bay. But it's just as well. On any given day, one could venture out to Jack London's restaurants, tourist shops, and beautiful marina without the parking hassles, crowds, and over-priced attractions that are mainstays over at Fisherman's Wharf.

On a cloudy afternoon in February, the sun was making its descent just as I pulled into the parking lot next to Jack London Village. Alyce sat quietly in the car beside me. It had been over a year since we'd first met, and within the last few months our relationship had become quite serious. Under different circumstances, this would have been great, but the fact that she was still married made our relationship fragile at best. Things had to change. I decided a quiet walk along the waterfront might help us sort things out.

We walked out by the water. Except for one or two other lone figures, there was virtually no one else around. We made our way down along the estuary, our pace was slow and deliberate. As we walked along a vacant strip of land next to the water, my eyes wandered through the murky blue waters of the bay, then off into the distant silhouette of San Francisco's jagged skyline. Soon the gray and blue horizon fell into the water and blackness coated the night. As we strolled the docks, water rippled and slapped noisily against the weathered planks.

Lights from nearby buildings sparkled in the water and reflected off the Alameda side of the bay. The air was crisp, and a chilly west wind blew in off the bay. Alyce wore a purple raincoat, a black felt hat, and leather gloves. I had on a brown, full-length overcoat. We walked to the end of the estuary and then back.

Then I was clear. I stopped, pulled her into my arms and kissed her. I told her I didn't care what it took, I wanted to be in that relationship to the end, to the box. In the past I'd always just fallen into whatever came my way but I didn't want to do that anymore. I'd never been able to trust in my previous relationships. I wanted to try and open up my heart and live honestly, to choose to accept beauty and love in my life. Her friendship, support, and love—had helped me grow tremendously. I told her I didn't care about our current circumstances, and that I didn't care what other people thought—I didn't want to lose her. She was the best thing that had ever happened to me.

That was the first time I'd ever said anything like that to a woman. I had always been too strong, which was my greatest weakness. This was the first time I let myself be vulnerable enough to ask for what I really wanted.

After that, we started seeing each other as often as possible. Since she was still married, it was a "Me and Mrs. Jones" thing. We'd meet for lunch one day, dinner the next. We'd usually meet at different spots around downtown Oakland after she got off work, spending brief moments together before she went home to her husband. Each time we got together it was an adventure, full of excitement, romance, and... emotional turmoil. Each time we'd meet, my guilt came up. Oh God, we can't do this, she's married. It's not right, I'd say to myself. We were in love, but we still didn't know what to do about it.

Finally, Alyce decided to leave her husband.

It was the end of spring, and I was still working at CareerCom. We were having a party for the Spring Graduation at a rooftop restaurant, downtown behind the Kaiser Building.

"It's going to be a big celebration and I want to show you off to my students," I told Alyce. "Meet me there."

When Alyce arrived at the party, I greeted her with a big hug and a kiss. There was no hesitancy. All of the ambivalence was gone. It was as if we were finally free to express our real feelings. We danced all night long and partied up a storm, and when it was all over, Alyce came home with me.

After that night, our relationship took off. We set a wedding date and began to make plans for our life together. Alyce has been there for me since the beginning of Simba—from the very first Simba orientation. Our relationship is like nothing I've ever experienced. She's always believed in me. Our love is like no other friendship of the spirit. Remember when you were a small child and your best friend came over and asked if you could come out and play? Remember that special feeling you had? That's me and Alyce. We're playmates. She's my best friend. We're at home together.

My vision for Simba was well on its way. The first chapter was established and the brothers had already gained the use of the *Oakland Post* building to hold meetings with the boys. As in every Simba chapter, they were responsible for recruiting all of the boys for their chapter. They had six boys who came regularly to the meetings.

One day I visited them at the *Oakland Post* to see how things were going. When I walked in, the men were doing a centering exercise with the boys. They had their chairs arranged in an arc formation. Six boys and three men sat with their hands palms-up on their laps, seemingly in perfect harmony and concentration. No matter how many times I've seen the boys centering, it always does something to me. Deep in concentration, they look like young African warriors preparing for battle. It is a powerful image, and in stark contrast to the image so often portrayed in the media—of young, angry black boys, strutting down city streets in gangs to rob, shoot, and kill each other over drugs. Sadly, that's all we ever see. When the men first found these boys, many of them were quickly on their way to fulfilling that image. But now, after a little more than a year in Simba, their transformation was obvious. It had been a long struggle, but the brothers in Chapter One had found a way to break through all of the negative clutter in their lives. They had taught the boys what they'd learned during the sixty-six hour training. As I sat and watched them meditate, I was overwhelmed with a sense of pride. The circle was complete.

"All right brothers, let's check your lifework," said Michael, a Simba leader.

All of the boys took out their journals and sat waiting for their work to be inspected. Michael walked around the arc and checked each boy's work.

"Leroy, Markel, and Milford, you're out of agreement. What happened?" he asked.

One by one, the three boys stood and explained their reason for not completing their lifework. Michael and the other men didn't say anything. Instead the other boys offered their support.

"Leroy, you said you finished your lifework but you left it at home, right?" asked Robert.

"Yeah, but I did do it," said Leroy.

"That's cool that you finished it, man, but it don't help you that you don't got it here now. I mean you came real close—but it don't count now," said Robert

"Naw, naw. It do count! I did it, I finished it!" protested Leroy.

"Well, where is it?" asked Robert.

"I told you, at home. My mom cleaned my backpack and she took my Simba journal out. So it wasn't in there this morning. But I did do it," Leroy protested.

"But judging by results, you didn't do it. We all remember the agreement, right? All lifework is to be presented at Simba in order for it to count. Remember?" asked Robert.

Leroy didn't answer.

"Leroy?"

"Yeah," mumbled Leroy.

"Leroy, how could you have been in agreement with your lifework?" asked Robert.

"I don't know," said Leroy.

"Even though you didn't have it with you when you got here, what could you have done?" asked Robert.

"I don't care! This is dumb! It doesn't matter, 'cause I did it!" shouted Leroy as he slumped down in his chair.

"You gave your word to your Simba brothers about your lifework. You made an agreement. When you don't keep that agreement you're not just letting us down, you're letting yourself down. Now if you want to remain a part of Simba, you have to be faithful to your word. Understand?" asked Charles, another Simba leader.

"Yes," said Leroy.

"Now your brothers are always going to be here for you.

When they ask you questions, they're trying to help you find new ways to beat your program, you know what I'm saying?"

"Yes."

"Well Leroy, what do you think you could have done different so that you'd be in agreement now?" asked Robert.

"I don't know. I... I guess I coulda asked for help."

"Asked who for help?"

"All y'all, my Simba brothers."

"What could you have said?"

"Well, I guess I coulda reneged my agreement."

"You mean renegotiated?"

"Yeah, that's it."

"How could you have done that?"

Leroy thought for a slow minute. All the boys watched him closely. Then, as if a light had gone on in his head, his eyes lit up and he smiled.

"I coulda just said I needed to call my mom, and then I coulda just asked her to bring it here to the meeting. That way I coulda proved to y'all that I finished it!" he said with a surprised smile.

Robert and the other boys all smiled, and the men congratulated Leroy for finding a solution to his problem. Then Milford and Markel were processed by the Simba boys in the same way. I watched with pride. The process really worked.

One of the biggest concepts I had taught the men during the Leadership Seminar was the deadly "Three R's." The Three R's are responsible for more broken friendships, failed marriages, suicides, murders, drive-by shootings, and even full-scale wars than anything else. They are: Resentment, Resistance, and Revenge. Our whole lives are spent in relationships. We are in relationships with ourselves, with others, with our environment, and so on. If something happens in one of those relationships that causes us to feel resentment, either towards ourselves or others, then we've already begun the cycle. Resistance and ultimately revenge will follow. The Three R's are a vicious cycle and the only escape from them is open, honest communication.

The boys in Simba Chapter One ranged in age from seven to thirteen. Many of them lived in the nearby Acorn housing projects and they fought everyday over the most petty issues.

At those tender ages, they had already become hardened by their environment. Revenge is almost common law in the ghetto, especially for males, so the Three R's was the first concept the men taught the boys.

That day, after a presentation on Malcolm X by one of the Simba leaders, the men took the boys out to the schoolyard to play ball. When we got outside, the boys split up and played a game of 3-on-3 basketball.

"Yo pass it," shouted Khadafy, a chubby eight-year-old.

"Watch me bust this nigga!" shouted Markel as he dribbled the ball down the court. He was guarded by Milford, who shuffled back and forth trying to stay with the older, taller boy.

"Pass it!" cried all the other boys on Markel's team.

"I got the shot. Take this boy!" said Markel as he bulldozed his way into Milford and threw up a brick that collided into the front of the rim.

"Foul! That's a foul! You fouled me!" protested Milford.

Just then Milford's little seven-year-old cousin, Jason, ran up and got in Milford's face.

"Ahhh! Milford! You got dogged! Ha, ha, ha, you ain't no good. Nya, nya, nya, nya nya!" taunted Jason.

Milford immediately darted after the little boy, chasing him all over the court, then slugging him hard in his back. The boy let out a loud scream and one of the Simba brothers rushed over to the scene.

"Milford! Jason! Come over here!" said Michael.

"He hit me first!" said Jason

"He won't stop messing with me!" cried Milford, still trying to kick Jason.

Michael separated the two boys, and sat Milford down on a bench.

"Milford, you feel something, right?" asked Michael.

"I'd kill him if I get my hands on him," said Milford.

"Milford, you can tell him, 'I want you to stop messing with me.' That's cool. That's responsible. There's nothing wrong with you telling him you're angry. If you fight him, what's going to come back to you?" asked Michael.

"Revenge," said Milford.

Leroy, who was watching the whole thing, walked by.

"You shoulda fired on him, Milford," he said.

"See? He wants you to be stuck in that program. It's not a matter of strength to fight. It's a matter of strength to find a solution. Get creative. You sit here and think about other ways you could have handled that situation, then come tell me. All right?"

"All right," said Milford.

Word was spreading about Simba. By the time I held the orientation for Simba Chapter Two, as many as twenty men signed up to go through the training. By the end of the summer of 1990, Simba Chapter Two had finished their Leadership Seminar and Chapter Three was just starting. I held the orientation and the seminar for Chapter Three at CareerCom. Somehow, the word about Simba got out on the local college campuses and several college students signed up for the training. Many of them had heard of Simba as a rites-of-passage group for black men and they were anxious to go through the process. During the orientation, I explained to them about the obligations of every Simba man:

"Every Simba Leader must complete the sixty-six-hour leadership training before they can work with boys and every man must be willing to make a twelve-year commitment to the boys in his chapter," I said.

As usual, there was resistance, but most agreed and we began the process. The men from the other chapters staffed during the seminar, so I had tremendous support and we finished the first forty hours right on schedule. Afterwards, I learned a valuable lesson. Many of the college students were "takers." They finished the forty hours of training and then moved away. Some graduated and took jobs in different cities; others just dropped out. During the intensive forty hours, they gained valuable tools to help them resolve emotional scars, lost love, anger, self-esteem issues, and many other negative programs. Empowered with this self-knowledge, the men were expected to give it back by working with the boys. But many of these young brothers just didn't get it. I can only hope that wherever they are, they're passing on Simba concepts to empower our people.

After I finished the Leadership Seminar for Simba Chapter Three, men began calling and leaving messages on the recruitment line, wanting more information about Simba. The

Simba brothers were telling others how the program had impacted their lives. Soon I had more than enough men ready and waiting to start new Simba chapters. This period was a turning point for me. I began to trust the process and move forward, regardless of the many obstacles I encountered. We held seminars for new chapters back-to-back, and although they were more manageable now, the issues that came up for the men during processing seemed to be getting more and more intense. We uncovered self-hate, uncontrollable anger, family violence, child abuse, and others that had been suppressed. During the seminar, the men began to get clear on why they were the way the were; it was all based on their childhood experiences.

Every time I do a seminar, I am healed. Whatever comes up for the men, whatever breakthroughs they make, affect me. When I'm processing other people, I'm processing myself. When I teach the material, I'm teaching it to myself. There's always at least one person in the seminar who's there for me. Their issues are my issues, and I wind up helping them resolve their issue while helping myself. After completing the seminar for Simba Chapter Four, something came up for me. I realized that I hadn't let go of Velma, my first wife. There was a part of me that still thought that maybe one day we'd get back together. Alyce and I had already gotten married and things were working well in our relationship, but I realized that this issue was preventing us from achieving that complete bond we wanted.

The day after the seminar, I sat down and I wrote Velma a letter. She hadn't been on my mind; she had just kind of snuck up on me and then I thought about her.

It was the hardest letter I've ever had to write in my life. I was letting her go, forgiving her, and forgiving myself. At the end of the letter, I wrote:

I will not find my future in my past. I have a new life. This is my future, this is what I choose, and I must let you go.

Then I threw it in the fireplace and watched it burn to ashes.

About two weeks later I happened to be in L.A. visiting my family and I decided to go visit my son, Roland. He had been arrested on burglary charges a couple of years earlier and was serving an eight-year sentence at a prison just outside L.A.

After Velma and I split up for good, I had done my best to stay in touch with my two sons, but I was still struggling, trying to turn my own life around. Meanwhile, they grew up like most ghetto kids, without the constant presence of a father.

When I arrived at the prison, it just so happened that Velma was there visiting Roland, too. In all the years my son had been incarcerated, his mother and I had never visited him together. It was a great experience. We got a chance to sit and talk and I got to tell her everything I was still holding on to. This meeting was just what we needed. I cried and told her how sorry I was about all the broken promises, lies, and violence. And it was as if she had gotten the letters. She understood and was very forgiving. After talking with her, I was able to completely let her go and move on with my life.

In the coming months, I began to make plans to train other men to be Simba instructors. I needed to teach the brothers everything I knew so our organization could continue to grow. Eventually, they would conduct seminars themselves and I'd be free to keep expanding my vision for Simba. The big question was: How do you teach black men to be vulnerable, supportive, and caring, and to remain so aware of their own programs that they're able to be totally there for the men in training? I knew that they'd have to experience a personal transformation in order to have something to give as teachers. I really didn't know how it would happen or how I would teach them, I just trusted the process and pressed on with my plans.

The first session of instructor's training took place on March 7, 1991, at the West Oakland Health Clinic. Sixteen people signed up for the training. All were Simba men with the exception of Alyce. Alyce eventually wanted to start a Simba program for African American women and girls. We agreed it would be necessary for her to start with the foundation of the instructor's training before she branched off and started Simba women's chapters. The training consisted of thirteen, three-hour, weekly meetings, plus three, eight-hour, all-day sessions, for a total of sixty-three hours of training time. I found two excellent books for the course: *Adult Children: The Secrets of Dysfunctional Families,* by John Friel & Linda Friel, and *Healing the Shame that Binds You,* by John Bradshaw. These two books addressed most of the issues common to many families, black

and white. But they were written for the white perspective. So
the most important thing I had to do was take them and
"culturize" them, to give them meaning from an African
American perspective. Bradshaw's book did an excellent job
on "disassociation through shame"—how we disassociate
ourselves from ourselves because of shame. And as a people,
African Americans are shame-based. We have been shamed
continuously throughout our history in this country.

In the beginning, the class thought they were going to
learn about some complex teaching technique or style.
However, they quickly discovered that they were there to learn
about themselves. The first thing an instructor must learn is
how to be completely conscious of what's going on with
himself, and then be totally there for the other person. If an
instructor is needy, then the participant is there for the
instructor.

Each time we met, I'd have them pair up and practice
processing each other on various life issues. During our first
Saturday, all-day session, I checked their lifework and was
surprised to find that they were out of agreement.

"Life is a series of tests, and you're about to undergo one.
Try not to resist the tests that life brings. Otherwise you may
wind up being in resistance to your life. If you don't do your
lifework, your programs will run your life," I said.

I had them split up into diads and begin a processing
exercise.

They learned how to observe body language, speech habits,
evasive behavior, and a variety of other elements of processing.
The main piece they had to learn was not to judge or
interrogate, but to be able to see beyond the mask, to see what
was really going on.

After the exercise, I had them regroup and sit in an arc
formation. One brother was missing. I was ready to begin
without him, when suddenly he ran in and took a seat. There
are rarely any valid excuses for being late. When someone is
late to a Simba meeting, it is usually a cry for help. Breaking
agreements are always a clear indicator that there's an issue
within that person that wants to be resolved, that they're asking
for help but they don't know how. This person knew he'd
have to explain why he was late to the group, but he offered
no excuses. He just waited for me to begin.

"Martin, please stand... Why did you set yourself up to fall?" I asked.

"Roland, I didn't plan to be late," he said.

"Come on, brother, you've been through the sixty-six hours, you know about agreements... you knew if you were late, you'd be standing right here, getting processed. Why did you choose to punish yourself today?"

We began going back into other areas of his life where he had set himself up to fail.

"What is it that you don't like about you?" I asked.

"I don't know what you're talking about. I like me."

"You like you, but you treat yourself like you don't. You set yourself up," I said.

He became very defensive, which told me I was headed in the right direction. So I began probing deeper. I didn't provide any answers. I knew he would provide those himself. I began to question him about his childhood, looking for buried issues. He was excited about the possibility of learning something about himself, yet still fearful of exposing himself in front of the group.

"Martin, let me talk to the other person, not the one who just says the defensive things. Face your fear, open up. Who hurt you when you were a child?" I asked.

He thought for a long time. I questioned him about his childhood relationships. When I asked about his relationship with his brother, I noticed his body starting to tremble. He became very uneasy. I knew I'd hit upon an issue. For the healing process, it was important for him to get it all out. I had to ask him everything.

"What happened?" I said.

"I was a victim of my brother. He... he raped me."

He broke down and began crying.

"How long did this go on?"

"For years," he sobbed.

"Did he rape you all that time?"

"Yes."

"How did you feel about it?"

He didn't answer.

"Did you help him?" I asked.

"What do you mean?"

"Tell me about it. Describe it."

He stood motionless in the middle of the arc, teary-eyed and breathing heavily. He was vulnerable and afraid, but he finally let go.

"We were home, alone, and I was in my room playing and my older brother came in and we started playing and wrestling. Then it just happened. He started messing with me. He held me down and took off my pants and did it to me," he explained.

"After that did you 'play' with your brother often?" I said.

"Yeah," he whispered.

As I continued to question him, it was clear that his relationship with his brother was a source of affection, love and warmth, which he hadn't been getting from his parents. When the sexual activity had started, he had been an eight-year-old, and he participated in it for several years until his older brother turned sixteen. Then it finally stopped.

His brother was the perpetrator, but Martin's anger was toward himself. As a part of the healing process, I needed to help him understand that at that young age, his participation was normal.

He had taken his adult perspective and put it on a nine-year-old, and he was unconsciously beating himself up over it.

"Who you were then and who you are now is two different people. It was not your fault. In order for you to get past this you must forgive yourself. Hey man, all the blame stops here, all the self-inflicted pain and anger stops right now. Martin are you ready to let it go?" I asked.

He was still looking down, obviously ashamed.

"Martin, can you see how this guilt program is running your life? It will make you feel unworthy and cause you to continue to sabotage yourself. In order for you to be able to train other men, you have to free yourself of this guilt or you'll pass it on. This is a part of your lifework and you can do it. It's a choice. You deserve it, Martin. You deserve it," I said.

This was an issue that hadn't come up for him during the leadership seminar. Since the instructor training was a smaller group with more advanced instruction, the degree of self-analysis was much more intense. After several hours of processing and group interaction, Martin began to get clear on what was going on with him and how to deal with it.

Six months later, I finished the instructor training. The

entire training had been a journey into self-discovery for all of us. It all came down to lifework. That was the single most important element I'd used in the training. When the men did their lifework—that is, when they took the time to observe themselves and study new techniques for inner growth and personal fulfillment—they thrived. And as a group we found the solution to many of our conflicts.

The Ghetto Solution is both an inspirational story and a black warrior's survival manual. It's a lesson and a warning,
lest any of us forget that we live in a
white, racist-controlled society where
smart-bombs are valued above smart
children, and where we are taught from
infancy to hate and distrust each other,
ourselves, and our heritage. The Ghetto
Solution shows how we so easily fall
victim to the white man's game... but
reminds us that it is ultimately our own,
individual decision to play.

—Jess Mowry
Author of Way Past Cool

Chapter 10

Power

"All 4 in King Beating Acquitted. Violence Follows Verdicts; Guard Called Out

Looting and Fires Ravage L.A.; 25 Dead, 572 Injured, 1,000 Blazes Reported"

—*excerpt from May 2nd issue of* Los Angeles Times

I was on my way to the dojo for my regular karate workout when the Rodney King verdict came blaring over my car radio. Instantly I felt hurt, anger, fear, outrage, and hopelessness... but not surprise. I had been prepared for this ever since the trial had been moved to Simi Valley. Actually, I had been prepared for it all my life. Injustice and brutality from white people towards black people is a documented fact of life, both historically and presently. The form may change, but the result remains the same.

Being verbally and physically abused by white policemen had been a normal part of life for me and for everyone else I knew, growing up in the Los Angeles ghetto. I'm sure the residents of South Central L.A. weren't shocked that Rodney King was brutally beaten by white policemen. But they were surprised that the subsequent injustice was so blatant.

If I'd been in my previous mindset (which I call the "African American Victim Program" and which I'll discuss in detail in the last chapter of this book) when I first heard the news, I would have gone straight into blame, then resentment, resistance, and revenge.

As it was, I took a deep breath, felt the pain and anguish, then exhaled and tried to let it all go.

I made my turn onto Telegraph Avenue and thought: At this very moment all of the people fighting, looting, burning, and dying do not know who they really are and that they have

the power to change their lives and their circumstances. They
do not understand that through blame and violence, they are
actually giving their power away to the very people they blame.
They do not know that they are settling for being right rather
than getting the results they truly want.

I knew that I would have to double my resolve and my
efforts to bring Simba to my people.

The next day, the news talked of riots, violence, and looting
spreading to many other major cities across the country.
Violence and looting erupted across the bay in San Francisco
and even in Berkeley. But not in Oakland. Angela Davis and
many other warriors from the turbulent sixties came out for a
rally on the steps of the Alameda County Courthouse. Black
folks set up non-violent protests and demonstrations, and
mobilized the community to take action. The consciousness
and memory of the Black Panthers is still strong in this city,
and many brothers and sisters still know how to organize
effectively against police brutality without becoming victims.
Less than twenty years ago, disciplined, uncompromising black
men, dressed in black leather jackets, black berets, and bearing
rifles, patrolled Oakland's city streets. The Panthers watch-
dogged the police and created a sense of racial family among
our people.

As I turned off the TV, I thought about those four police
officers. As hard as I tried, I couldn't rationalize their treatment
of King. Worse yet was the jury's verdict. How could they not
see their own racism? I could only answer that many white
people must not understand or even recognize their own racism.
It is as much a part of them as their favorite foods, their
politics, and their religion, yet they don't see it. Their racism is
a living, breathing organism, that has insidiously grown and
evolved over hundreds of years; it has become a blind giant
within the American consciousness. So, it's no accident that
seminars on racial conflict and resolution have become ever-
present fixtures in Oakland's politically charged community.

Two weeks after the King verdict, I heard about such a two-
day seminar being held at Merritt College. I knew this would
be a great opportunity for a few newly trained Simba instructors
and me to gain more insight into America's race problem and,
hopefully, learn something to give to the boys.

When I arrived Saturday morning, about two hundred people were gathered in a big room. In the center of the room was a huge brick fireplace with four chairs arranged around it, facing the group of people. A small white man stood in front of the group talking. He was Dr. Ronald Clark, a renowned activist and psychologist active in the world of conflict resolution. Dr. Clark stepped up to the podium. "The first step to conflict resolution is awareness. The only way for an awareness to develop is through communication. We have to talk to each other! This is how we will resolve this race issue," he said.

He walked over to the fireplace and grabbed two chairs. He sat them in the middle of the room, about two feet apart, facing each other.

"This exercise will help us see some of the dynamics going on in our perceptions of each other. I need two volunteers for the role-playing: one white, middle-class American who doesn't want to give up his privileges to allow more opportunity and equal treatment of African Americans, and an African American person who will argue the other point-of-view," he said.

A black man walked down the aisle from the back of the room where he'd been sitting quietly and took a seat in one of the chairs.

"All right! Now all we need is another. Who will it be?" asked Dr. Clark.

No one came forward.

"There has to be someone." said Dr. Clark.

A black woman stood up.

"I know somebody here who can play the other role. I mean, he might not have to play a role, just step up and be himself," she said.

A tall, skinny, red-haired man got up from the pillow he was sitting on and walked down the aisle.

"I'll play," he said, sitting down in front of the black man.

"Great, I knew we could do this!" said Dr. Clark.

"Hi, brother. My name is Ted," said the red-haired man, extending his hand.

"How you doing? I'm David," said the brother.

"Brothers, keep in mind that although this is role-playing, there has to be a part of you that agrees with the stance that you take. Be real and trust the process. Don't be afraid to say anything or act out your feelings... let it all out! Now, here's how this works. I'll introduce a topic on race and you just begin discussing your points of view on it. Have a regular conversation," said Dr. Clark.

He walked over to the microphone, which sat atop a podium in the middle of the room between the two men.

"The topic is power," he said.

The men began discussing all of the implications of power within the races and how it has been used to discriminate against some, while helping others. The longer they talked, the more heated the conversation became.

"White corporate America is completely out of touch with the race problem in this country. You don't understand what I have to go through as a black man, what I have to sacrifice, in order for me to make it in this country," said David.

"Maybe I don't understand, but this *is* America and you have it just as bad and as good as the rest of us. I mean, I realize you do have discrimination to deal with, but don't we all have some sort of obstacle to overcome?" said Ted.

"Maaan, I know you're not serious. Wake up! Look, the white power structure in this country has kept the black man locked out or locked down since day one. Just being white, you innately have more privileges and opportunities than all other people of color, especially African Americans," said David.

"I don't know what you mean by the 'white power structure,' but I do know that you're afforded the same opportunities in this society as I am. I mean, again I'm aware of the disadvantages black people face, but the opportunities are still there for those of you who work hard."

"Check this... A black man defines himself through his ability to be successful in this country. If he isn't working because his opportunities for work have been cut off and he can't provide for his family, he has failed what for him is probably his first test of manhood. Racism is the oldest thing going in this country, next to capitalism, and it continues to hold the black man back."

Ted didn't say a word.

"Do you see what I'm saying?" asked David.

"Well, yes and no. I mean, yes I agree with you on the historical perspective of racism, but we've evolved beyond much of that as a nation. A lot of what you say no longer applies. America is a nation of immigrants as diverse as you'll find anywhere. And each group has a burden to bear," said Ted.

"Immigrants, huh? Well I guess that might apply to the people who came to this country voluntarily, but for the millions of Africans enslaved and forcibly brought to this country in the hulls of slave ships, the word 'burden' takes on a whole new meaning. You just don't get it do you?"

"Look—my point is that we've all suffered. I'm Jewish. My people almost faced genocide and over six million were exterminated, wiped out... so don't talk to me about not understanding!"

"OK. So you see what I'm talking about. You understand. Now understand *this*—before the Holocaust, before the Native Americans, before the Chinese Americans, and before the destruction of any other race of people on this earth, the African man had caught hell. We are the original people, the creators of world civilization, and so we were the first to be envied and despised for our greatness... six million people? You're sad? You're hurt? You're angry? Man, over forty million of my African brothers and sisters didn't even make it to this living hell. FORTY MILLION! You know anything about the Middle Passage, brother? Check it out. Then come talk to me... Forty Million! That's more than the total African American population in this country today! Generations of beautiful, black living souls, gone just like that!" he said.

A white school teacher stood up and began defending the Jewish viewpoint. Then everyone joined the feud. Folks hopped out of their chairs and started yelling to be heard. An Asian man stood up and started yelling at a white man. Two middle-aged white women ran out of the room. A young blonde woman, no more than twenty-two years old, ran up to the brother in the chair. She began pleading with him.

"I'm sorry my ancestors enslaved your people! I didn't know it was that bad! I didn't know! Forgive me! Forgive me! Please forgive me," she sobbed.

I couldn't believe my eyes. The whole room was completely polarized. Down in front, the whites were on one side and the blacks were on the other. Everyone was speaking but no one was listening. As I sat in the back watching it all, I figured that these people were either the best actors I'd ever seen or all those years of being nice and phony and pretending that race wasn't an issue had finally come to a boiling point. It was utter chaos.

All of a sudden a brother stood up and began screaming.

"People! My people! Let us not forget to love! In the midst of all this, let us not forget to love!" he said.

And then you could hear a pin drop. No one moved. It was as if his words had doused the fire. Then, without saying a word, a young black man got up and walked to the podium. It was Chris Billups, a Simba instructor.

"What's going on here? What are we doing? I mean... are we in a contest to see who's the world's biggest victim? I feel that most of the black people here are trying to get their power from white people. My experience is this... as long as we think white people have all of our power we won't accomplish anything. We'll always be the victim. We don't get what we want by persecuting white people for not giving us what they don't have. They don't have our power," he said.

Still sitting in the chair, David turned to Chris.

"Brother, we're talking about innate privileges that all white people have in this society, and we're talking about getting some of those same privileges and power for black people," he said.

"David, can't you see that you're giving away your power? As soon as you say that we can't get it or that the white man has to give up his privilege in order for us to get it, then you don't have no power," said Chris. Then he put the mike down and walked over to his seat, and sat down next to Keith. A few people clapped.

People began to get up and Dr. Clark was instructing everyone to go home and get clear on what had just happened.

"The conference will resume tomorrow at 9 a.m. See you then," he said.

As we headed for the door, a white woman stopped us. She wanted to talk with Chris.

"Excuse me. Hi, my name is April Lewis. I'm really happy you're here. I was very impressed with what you were saying. We're going to be having another conference like this in Switzerland, and we'd like you to come. Is there a way you think you could make it?" she asked.

Chris explained that he didn't have much money, but Ms. Lewis was later able to solicit some anonymous donations to sponsor both Chris and Keith's participation in the Swiss conference.

Word spread fast to the men in the other Simba chapters about Chris and Keith's upcoming trip. They were the youngest men to become Simba instructors. Both were under twenty-five and very enthusiastic. They had helped recruit many of the college students for Simba Chapter Three.

When they received their tickets in the mail, it was official. I was so proud of them. They had come so far from the angry, afraid young men I'd met during the leadership seminar for Simba Chapter Two. The day before they were to leave for the conference, I took them out to dinner and drinks at Mexicali Rose, a well-known spot downtown.

By the time we had finished eating, it was late and the restaurant was almost empty. A busboy cleaned the table across from us as a waitress swept the floor. We sat at a table in the corner and talked.

"This will be a great opportunity for you to see and observe people from all over the world. You will be among a select few African Americans to witness what really goes on at these world conflict/resolution conferences and you won't be far from the United Nations—where it all happens. Observe the human issues. Remember, as African Americans, we were taught to think like white people. You must get out of that count and measure mode. Don't segment your thinking by looking for the differences among the people you meet. Find the similarities. Keep an Afrocentric focus, but stay centered on the human issues. They're the most important," I advised.

As we sat in the restaurant talking about saving our people and telling the world about Simba, I couldn't help but feel enormous pride and love for these two young men. They'd come so far in such a short time.

And yes, they were ready.

The next day, when their plane landed in Zurich, they headed for the gate. They had to pass through two booths where customs agents checked their identification.

"I need your passport," said a German man.

Chris opened his wallet and showed him his passport.

Keith did the same. Then they gathered their bags and continued to the next booth. Chris quickly passed through, but as Keith entered the booth, a tall, blonde man stepped in his way.

"Stop! How did you get here?" he asked.

"I came off the plane," said Keith.

The small booth was barely big enough for both men to share. The white man looked angry and stood with his hand open, demanding identification from Keith.

Keith showed him his I.D. and his passport.

"Is this normal? I mean do you ask everyone who comes here where they came from. Or just the black people?" Keith asked.

The whole booth filled up with energy and the man got red in the face.

"OK. Everything is in order. Thank you," he said as he handed Keith his passport.

Keith hurried out of the booth and caught up to Chris, who stood waiting on the other side.

"What was that all about?" asked Chris.

"That, my brother, was the Welcoming Committee!" said Keith.

That night they stayed with a host family, and the next morning they caught a train to Stuss, where the conference was to be held.

The conference was held at a ski lodge. Over forty countries were represented and more than three hundred people were in attendance. After they checked in, Chris and Keith found their room. It was a small room with several cots on the floor. There were about twenty other black men in the room and they were from all over the world. There wasn't one white face to be found in the room.

Many of the same people who had attended the racial conflict resolution seminar in Oakland were there. Dr. Clark was also present, leading many of the sessions. Each day, Chris and Keith attended several meetings on conflict resolution and group dynamics. The meetings were held in a big hall with vaulted ceilings and gothic-looking architecture. One afternoon, everyone met there to discuss race conflict and what could be done about it from a world perspective.

Over three hundred people sat in a big circle. Just about every race of people was represented. Dr. Clark and his wife led a discussion on world race conflict.

They walked around with microphones and got people to form small focus groups where each person learned exercises to act out aggressions, attitudes, and beliefs about their perception of people different from themselves. Some people were shouting at each other, while others were jumping around, acting out mock aggression. There was a man in Chris and Keith's circle who was having trouble expressing his feelings about black people.

"Go ahead, Tomas, you can do it. We all acted out what we felt, it's your turn," said a Chinese woman.

"I don't know how to say this...I mean my feelings towards blacks are kind of uncomfortable to say," he said.

"Tomas, you don't have to say them, you can act them out," said Dr. Clark.

"I know but I... I don't know where to start," Tomas said.

"Start at the beginning," said a small woman. "When did you first develop these feelings towards black people?" she added.

"I'm not sure. I guess when I was a small child." said Tomas.

"OK now Tomas, I want you to trace your feelings. I'm going to help you get clear. I'll say a word and you tell me the first thing that pops into your mind. Remember self-honesty is the first step to awareness... Ready?" said Dr. Clark.

"Yeah," said Tomas.

"African," said Dr. Clark.

"Savage," said Tomas.

"Slave," said Dr. Clark.

"Dumb."

"Nigger," said Dr. Clark.

"Lazy."

"Negro," said Dr. Clark.

"Lazy."

"Black," said Dr. Clark.

"Dirty"

"African American," said Dr. Clark.

"Ugly."

"That's great Thomas, tell me more. Act that out. I want you to 'be' how you think black people are. Walk around the room. Be that. Be what your concept of black people is." said Dr. Clark.

Tomas was apprehensive. But slowly he began to walk like an animal. His face was contorted and his arm was over his head, scratching the side of his face. First he walked like a gorilla then he began to shuffle and make animal noises. He became all of the adjectives he used to describe Black people; dumb, lazy, ugly, etc. As he put on his show, his actions were slow and unsure, but soon he hit his stride and fell into rare form. He began to moan and groan and gradually got louder until people from other groups started to notice him. They came over to watch. Dr. Clark stretched his arms out towards Tomas and pushed his own "energy field" towards him.

"Fight it! Fight it! Get it out! You can destroy this belief Tomas! Fight it!" shouted Dr. Clark.

Tomas began to scream. He was yelling and pushing, fighting to let go of his deep beliefs about black people. Keith and Chris and the other African American people who were there that day watched it all in disbelief. Dr. Clark's therapy was definitely experimental, but it had merits. It allowed people to see just how deep their beliefs ran.

In the other group encounters that followed, the purpose of the conference became very clear. Many of the group exercises encouraged conflict, but then failed to resolve it. In many ways, it was just like the racial conflict/resolution seminar in Oakland. During one of the sessions, when things began to heat up between the races, people started assuming responsibility for other people. They didn't have the knowledge of being responsible *to* people rather than *for* them, that we teach in Simba. So people brought up the same old "victim" arguments and chose to assume other peoples' guilt or anger.

A few days before the conference was over, the fighting had gotten so bad that Keith and Chris stopped going to some of the classes. Instead, on their last day in Switzerland, they decided to tour the city. During their outing, they ran in to some of the same racism and prejudice that was so familiar back in the states.

Back in Oakland, we had a meeting and they filled me in on their experience in Switzerland.

"Roland, Dr. Clark is good at working with large groups. He gets people to tap into their real emotions, but he and his staff don't do enough "clean up," said Chris.

"That's right, they get people conscious of all their programs, but then there isn't enough one-on-one counseling to help them heal," added Keith.

Switzerland had opened them up to a new world of

knowledge. As two young, black males, they'd been exposed to more human issues than most men twice their age. They learned that things like race, religion, gender, sexual orientation, physical ability, and all the other ways we segment ourselves, are just ways to keep us from discovering who we really are, in a spiritual sense. Once again, they had done me proud.

The personal progress that Chris and Keith had made over the past year was phenomenal. Like many African American boys, they both had had somewhat tragic childhoods. During the Leadership Seminar for Chapter Two, when I first met them, I had begun to see firsthand how some of our young, black men are desperately searching for manhood.

I was doing a presentation on human issues versus other issues and I noticed that some of the brothers weren't paying attention. Some were writing in their notepads, others were watching each other. Chris stood up. He had something to share with the other brothers in the room.

"I just want to let everyone know I think it would be best if we all sat and focused on a brother when he's talking, instead of devoting our attention to other things," he said.

"Chris, please remain standing. Who criticized you when you were young?" I said.

"What?" he asked.

I walked over to him.

"Who criticized you when you were young?"

He didn't understand where the question came from and it threw him for a minute.

"Chris, when you were a child, growing up, who criticized you?" I asked.

"My mom criticized me," he said finally, his voice cracking.

"Well, can you go back in your mind and recall what she would say?"

"She'd say she wished I was more this way or more that way."

"More like what?"

"She'd say, uhm... she'd say, 'You should be more like Felipe'—my cousin."

"How did that make you feel?"

All eyes were on Chris. He was trembling and near tears.

"I don't know. I guess, uhm... I guess like, like she didn't like me very much," he said, wiping the tears from his face.

As I talked to him, I realized that someone else in the arc was crying. I looked at the name tag. It was Felipe, Chris's cousin.

Chris took a few deep breaths and continued.

"I guess she compared me to him because he focused in school and got good grades. He's from Tanzania and he speaks three languages, and he never, ever got in trouble like I did," he said.

I stood directly in front of Chris.

"Chris, the truth is that everybody is a unique individual. We all have special qualities." I said as I gave him a hug.

The next day I noticed another young man in the seminar, Keith. He was like many young brothers I had seen on many college campuses across the country. He was young, black, proud, and believed that his identity was in Africa. He wore African clothing and had an African medallion around his neck. This brother was down for African American people!

Most of the time I've seen people like that standing up haranguing a crowd, shouting, "Power to the People." When I began processing Keith, his issues started to come out clearly. He was a young man who was confused about his identity.

First of all, he was late, not in agreement, and I began to process him.

"Ah, I see you're wearing an African medallion. I really love those things. Where did you get it?" I asked.

"I got it from Marcus Books over on Martin Luther King," he said

"Oh, OK. So you're down for black people, huh?"

"Yeah."

I rose from my chair and began walking toward Keith, who stood in front of his chair.

"What do you think is most important for black people to understand these days?" I asked.

"Well, I think its important that we know who we are. We have to study our history. The Motherland is our home and we need to be about serving it and each other. It all comes down to unity, you know," he said.

"Ah, unity? Well... interesting. Is that why you're here going through this training? To develop unity with your brothers?"

"Yes. And I'm here to give something back to black boys."

That's what I'd been waiting to hear. I took a step closer looked him square in the eyes.

"Oh, so what are you going to teach them? That their word don't mean shit? That they're not responsible for what they do?"

"What do you mean? My word means a lot to me. I tried to get here on time. I missed my bus. I thought about catching a cab but I didn't have enough money. I took some action, I didn't just try to be late."

"Keith you made an agreement with me and the other men. You gave your word that you'd be here at 6 p.m., right?"

"Right, but..."

"OK, judging by results, were you here at 6 p.m.?"

"No, but..."

"So judging by results, what does your word mean?"

"No, it's not like that, my word is important to me. Everybody fails sometime. I mean I tried to get here on time. I missed my bus and then I was going to call a friend to see if he'd bring me here, but then I didn't have his number and..."

He was analyzing the whole situation, justifying his lateness to himself and trying to convince me and the other men of his sincerity. But he was missing the whole point.

"Keith... Don't you know it's because of men like you that our children are on the streets? You give them your word and then you let them down. And you're supposed to be one of the good ones? Now who's responsible for you being out of agreement here?"

He didn't answer.

I stepped up to him and grabbed his medallion.

"What are you going to teach black children? They learn what they see, not what you say. What are you going to teach them!?"

He got the message. Still holding his medallion, I turned my attention to the other men in the seminar.

"You know, brothers, to know our history and to not know ourselves, means we're still lost. We're even worse lost. If we know ourselves, then we can discover our history. If we have an understanding of how we think, feel, and act, then we can make agreements and keep them. We can build relationships based on choice and not fear. But if we don't know ourselves, our inner spiritual, emotional, and psychological selves, then our history simply becomes another piece of information."

When I looked at Keith I saw a "human doing," rather than a human being. A human doing always has so much pain that they're covering by doing. What he was saying in his rhetoric was much different from what he was portraying and teaching in his lifestyle. He would talk about unity for black people, but the way he lived and what he did had no unity in it.

Over the next two years I watched Keith and Chris take giant steps towards manhood. After they finished their seminar, they had a whole new outlook on life and wanted to continue their training. They enrolled in the training for Simba instructors. Several months later, when they graduated, they were two of the youngest men to ever complete the instructor's training. They came to me and said they were ready to teach their first seminar. I'd already recruited enough men to start a new Simba chapter, so I decided to step back and give these eager young brothers a chance. They led the entire seminar and I assisted them. It was a new experience for me and it gave me a chance to sit back and watch my model for Simba grow.

Chapter 11

Simba's Young Lions

Today Keith and Chris are two of the strongest leaders in Simba. Their personal growth as black men and Simba instructors has been tremendous. They know better than anyone else how Simba has affected their lives, so I'm going to let them tell their own stories.

Chris Billups, 24, Simba Instructor
I was born in Los Angeles and raised in Detroit until ninth grade. After that, I moved back to L.A. and graduated from Culver City High School. After high school, I went to the University of California at Berkeley. That's where I met Keith. We knew there was something we wanted to get accomplished for black people and for ourselves, so he and I and a couple other brothers started meeting on campus, trying to form a black-male support group. We had several meetings, and when the semester was over, the group just kind of faded out. I went home for the summer. When I came back, Keith told me about Simba.

We knew it was a group that was about helping African American men so we went to an orientation to learn more about the program.

Roland was wearing blue jeans, a white shirt, and some cream-colored loafers. I thought he looked odd. He didn't fit my stereotype of what I thought a black leader should look like. I expected him to look more militant. I thought he'd be wearing some African attire or maybe red, black, and green or something. I also noticed he was light skinned.

After I went through the first forty hours of the seminar, I thought it was some pretty serious stuff. I knew I wanted to know and do more. And I was amazed by Roland's on-pointness and his focus on what he does. He still amazes me today.

During the training, things got very real. I mean there was too much realness in his voice, and realness in peoples' perceptions of what he was saying, so I knew it wasn't a bunch of psycho-analytical bullshit. I bought into the whole thing right away.

A week after the first forty hours of the Leadership Seminar, I realized that I wasn't in love with my girlfriend. I realized I had a co-dependency issue with her. One day we got in an argument and she wanted to leave and end the relationship. I didn't want to be without this woman. I didn't want to be alone. I just wanted her to stay. She had been staying with me and I was talking about our ending living together, but she was talking about ending the relationship. We were sitting in my bedroom. At the time, I was taking architecture in school and I had drafting paper and architecture supplies sitting on the table. She was telling me that she was tired of the relationship and I was arguing that I would change, and that I had been trying, but it seemed like she didn't give me credit. But she didn't listen.

We started yelling at each other. I walked over to my desk and grabbed an exacto knife, flipped it up, and just started cutting my left wrist. Then I ran to the bathroom and closed and locked the door. She followed me.

I went to the sink and started cutting. Then I walked back out and showed her. She grabbed my wrists and then went to the phone to call 911. I ran out of the apartment and down the street a couple of blocks. I ran out because I knew if the cops came it would turn into a bigger deal than I wanted it to be. In retrospect, I was just intending to be dramatic. I had cut my wrists, but not badly enough for me to die. My motive was to get attention, I thought that maybe she'd hold on to me or something like that.

Later, the police found me and took me to Highland Hospital, and I remember looking around and thinking: "This is not a place where people get well." They gave me some gauze, put cuffs on my wrists, and took me to the psychiatric ward. It had a big metal door and the cops had to leave their guns behind because some of the people inside might try to grab them. They left me in a room with a brother who was talking crazy, pacing back and forth. After that a doctor came in and asked me questions.

Weeks later, as I finished up my Simba training, I came to

realize that I had a fear of abandonment and a shame issue. I had wanted attention and had done this to get it. After I finished the Leadership Seminar, I immediately knew I wanted more. Keith and I had always wanted to do something together and this was something we both felt passionate about. We decided to take the instructors seminar and learn as much as we could, then teach seminars together. When I started my instructor training, a lot of fear came up for me. I questioned my competency. I felt that maybe I wasn't smart enough to be an instructor, partly because the processing in the instructor's training was point-blank range. Questions are asked straight, no-chaser, and it was intense. When we finished, I was overjoyed, just happy to be through with all that stuff. I went through a lot of emotional pressure sitting in a room all those hours, listening to people and watching them make mistakes, making mistakes myself, and finally learning that it was OK.

The biggest thing about the instructor's seminar, to me, is finding out your life's purpose. I began to question myself and ask if this is really what I wanted to do. In March, 1990, I decided to stop going to school and do what I really liked doing, working as a Simba Instructor.

Afterwards, Keith and I talked about eventually getting paid and teaching our own seminar. We went to Roland and told him we were ready to teach, ready to do our own chapter. He met with us and took us through the manual. Then we did a seminar for Simba Chapter Five. Chapter Five had about seven men. During the seminar, two things really happened for me. I learned to let go of my need-to-be-right program and my criticism program. The biggest thing that came up for me as an instructor was my age. Some of the brothers in the seminar were twice my age and I had to tell them their shit stank. All types of personal, "father-figure" stuff came up for me. I realized halfway through the process that they were trusting us. Nothing glued them in the chair, they could've left any time they wanted to. They stayed because they were getting something, and it was working. I thought many of these older brothers were great for trusting people half their age.

Simba has given me an awareness of some of my weaknesses and it empowered me with knowledge that I could use to change them. I also learned that I can help other people change their programs. I learned that as a people, we don't have to settle for less. It woke me from sleeping while my foot was on fire. As a whole, black peoples' houses are on fire and we're asleep. The concepts in Simba have given me a new outlook.

For example, it's allowed me to now be in a relationship with a woman and not seek revenge for stuff that she has nothing to do with. I now take full responsibility for my actions. I am engaged to be married and I am faithful. I am not co-dependent. It's allowed me to learn to love me more, and accept myself, regardless of mistakes I've made. I've learned to compare myself less. I've learned to be more honest and share real feelings. As far as my relationship with other brothers, I now have a group of people that I can turn to at any time and ask for support, cry on their shoulder, whatever. I like to look at us as a big "black mob," out to save our people. Some brothers talk about rolling thirty deep. In Simba, I'm rolling over a hundred deep and we're growing more everyday.

Keith Ragsdale, 25, Simba Instructor

When I was growing up, my father was not around. I had one brother and three older sisters. My mother was an alcoholic and she had a drug problem. She behaved like she didn't want to be in the ghetto. My interpretation of that was that she didn't want to be with me. She tried to kill herself several times. We saw her set herself on fire, more than once. One time after she'd been drinking, she put her hand and arm over the burner of the stove. We stopped her, but not before she had second- and third-degree burns on her wrists and arms. My mother wasn't one to hold her tongue and sometimes she would get drunk and have fights with my uncle. I thought my mother would kick even the devil's ass if he said something wrong to her. She just wasn't afraid to die. She had a very large energy, and when I was a kid, she seemed like a giant to me, even though she was no more than 5'2".

When I was eleven years old, my mother was killed in a fire. This split up the family. My sisters went to Colorado to live with their father's mother. My brother and I had a different father so we went to stay with relatives on my mother's side. My cousin became my legal guardian and I grew up with her.

The fire happened on a Saturday, January 20, 1979. I was watching TV in my room. My sister came in and asked me to make breakfast. I walked into the kitchen and there was smoke coming from the back porch. My sister ran in and said, "Mom's in there!" Then I heard my mother scream. The door to the back porch was missing a door knob and it was locked. So my sister got a spoon and opened the door. Big thick, black clouds of smoke came out and I could see the flames. My sister and I both ran out to get help from the next-door neighbor.

We were only gone maybe about two minutes. But by the time the neighbors had gotten to my house, there was a big explosion. It was the water heater and/or the stove. My mother's boyfriend and some other people rushed to the house. When he kicked down the door, the flames rushed out. The fire quickly spread throughout the house, then it burst through the roof.

Then the firemen began to arrive. I stood outside and watched. I began to realize that mom wasn't coming out of the house. I was scared and I didn't know what would happen. It was overwhelming to walk back into the house after the fire was out. The TV that I'd been watching had melted.

When I went back to school a friend of mine came up to me asking me a whole lot of questions. I told him about the fire and he started shaking his head saying, "See man, if that was me, I'd of had to go back in there. I'd of saved my mother," he said.

It had never occurred to me about saving her. A couple days later, I began to feel some guilt about not getting my mom out.

When I graduated from high school, I was emotionally distraught. I "adopted" many of my friends' moms. Since my mom died when I was real young, I never experienced having real arguments and teen-age problems with her. So I tripped when my friends would have problems with their mothers. I had about three of four "moms" during high school. After high school, I was tired of school. I didn't really care where I went. I met a recruiter from U.C. Berkeley and he came down and told me about college. My grades were good, so I got accepted to U.C. Berkeley. I left my guardian and I was happy to leave. I'd never felt like I had a home since the fire.

When I went to Berkeley I realized I was running away from a lot of pain. When I walked on campus I thought I was "Mr. Black." But understand, "Mr. Black" had no connection with Africa. Don't even go there! You got the wrong man! But I knew it all. Whenever a man called me brother, I was like, I hope he means black brother, 'cause I ain't African. One day, somebody came up to me and told me about a brother on campus who was giving a lecture. I went. He was an Egyptologist and he did two slide presentations on African history. One was on the "African Beginnings of Civilization" and the other was on the "African Beginnings of Judeo-Christianity." His presentation showed me pictures of stuff that I'd never seen and if he'd just said it, I would never of believed it, but he had slides and pictures. He took my Bible and showed me passages and pictures of Egypt. I was shocked. To me, my Bible fell out of the sky printed. I had never questioned it. Then I knew and understood that I was African and I was proud. But I was also very angry because I'd been fooled. Everybody knew. Why didn't anybody tell me? How could I have been ignorant for so long? Then I picked up Malcolm X's autobiography. Then I was really angry. I had gotten the book in junior high school, but because he was that evil "hate man," I hadn't read it. So after all these revelations I became "Mr. Africa."

Then one of the brothers brought a Simba flyer to a meeting on campus. The flyer said "rites-of-passage" training. Well, I had never been "initiated" or nothing like that and this was an initiation into manhood. I looked at the date, and I went to the orientation. At the orientation, I was blown away by how serious and focused the men were.

The training was incredible. I learned many things about myself and why I acted the way I did. My big issue had always been self-judgment, especially about my mom. I have been unwilling to forgive myself for her death. It became clear to me that if I forgave myself for what happened to her, it would mean that I didn't love her. So in order for me to love her, I needed to feel bad about not saving her. But after the training, man, I thought I could fly.

I knew I had a choice in everything I did. I felt really empowered. Even my friends could see the difference, and it was helping me with my relationships.

Next, I took the Simba instructor training. I realized I still had a lot of guilt over my mom, which I didn't know I still carried. One day, I was out of agreement, and Roland questioned me. I began to describe the scene where the boy asked me about my mother and I started to cry. Roland said, "You been carrying that around for eleven years?"

"I was supposed to save her," I said.

"Keith, you can't expect an eleven-year-old to know what to do in a situation like that. You did the best that you could do. And you weren't responsible for her. You went to get help and that was good. That was the best you knew how."

After that, I realized that I had to let it go and start living my life without blaming or judging myself.

I grew up in the ghetto and for a long time I had a ghetto state of mind and spirit. Simba has allowed me to choose how I think and to change what I believe about myself and my people. My life's purpose is to teach—to use what I've learned to help our children.

Chapter 12

Simba Women

Since I started Simba, I knew we would eventually develop a women's seminar, but I didn't know when or how. Now that Alyce had completed her Master's degree in counseling, it was time to make it a reality. A few weeks before, she had held an orientation for women interested in working with African American girls. Several women showed up, and we had enough names to start not one, but two Chapters for women. Their names were taken and the dates were set. The first Simba women's leadership seminar was set for two weeks after Alyce's graduation. Her opportunity to work with black women had finally come and she was ready to take it and run.

I've always known that I couldn't do the women's seminar. I wanted Alyce to do it. The biggest question that remained for Alyce was: How does the training need to be changed so it addresses the needs of black women? After much thought, she came to me and told me that the more that she analyzed it, the more it became clear to her that I needed to be in the seminar with her. She said one of the major issues that African American women have is African American men. She explained to me that many of our sisters are conditioned to think they don't need African American men and many of them have some deep-seated resentments towards brothers. This was news to me. I hadn't realized so many sisters held so much anger over their relationships with black men.

So together, as husband and wife, we conducted the very first Simba Women's Leadership seminar. At the final circle ceremony, at the end of the first forty hours of the seminar, we were very happy. It had worked. After helping Alyce do the women's seminar, I learned that black women have very different issues from men. Their pain is different, but just as devastating, if not more so.

Parallel to my own journey into self-discovery, my wife, Alyce, has also made strides and overcome tremendous odds to fulfill her greatness. As an African American woman, her early life experiences are tragically common, but her struggle and victory to overcome the odds against her is quite unique. Here in her own words, Alyce tells her story:

On September 4, 1984, I looked out the car window thinking I'd been up since 5:00 a.m. My mind was mentally creating a check list... tickets, passport, itinerary, French-English books... somehow I knew I had everything I needed for the trip, but this was really just an exercise to block out my feelings.

As the car moved along Highway 880, I saw a reflection of myself in the side mirror of the car. I looked directly into my eyes and for a moment the sadness I saw there caught me off guard. The look became a stare and I found my eyes staring back into my soul. A deep sense of fear moved from my chest up into my jaw. I took a deep breath and clenched my teeth, holding back a wave of emotions I was not ready to let go of, at least not now. I looked over in the driver's seat where my husband was sitting and another wave of emotions moved from my stomach up into my chest. I took another deep breath, which created a loud sigh upon release. I hated these moments of silence. I always felt a need to talk, a need to connect. Somehow this morning, I really needed to talk, and yet I knew if I did, my emotions would overwhelm me. I looked away from my husband and saw the signs of the Oakland Airport along the roadside. My husband quickly found a parking space. I always travel light—a small suitcase to fit under the seat and a travel tote handbag. My husband took the small suitcase and we hurried through the parking lot to the terminal. I looked upward to the sky. It was absent of clouds and the warmth of the sun gave me comfort... it was going to be a good day for travel.

Inside the terminal, I looked for the gate of departure for my flight and took off toward the gate with my husband following close behind. We arrived at the security check-in counter and had no trouble getting through security. At the gate, passengers for the flight were lining up to board the plane. My husband took me in his arms, kissed me, and wished me a safe trip. As he let go of me, my knees began to weaken, creating a wave of emotions that began to shake my body. I turned away from him, picked up my suitcase and walked through the doors leading to the airplane. I found my window seat and sat down. I leaned back into the seat and closed my eyes, I could feel the warmth of the sun through the window on my face. I thought if I don't open my eyes now I will be OK and the emotions will level off somewhere in my body. I was aware of the heaviness on my chest so I took some deep breathes but the heaviness became heavier... I couldn't stop my emotions from coming up. I could feel the warmth of tears on my face. I tried to hold my eyes tighter, but that didn't help, and the tears began to flow down my cheeks until they met at the corner of my mouth.

I didn't believe I was crying out loud until I heard those sounds coming out of my mouth. My chest was getting heavier and I was getting angry at myself for crying. What was crying going to do for me now? I was angry at my husband. I had wanted him to take this vacation trip with me. He had promised me a vacation—without business being the major focus of the trip. He hadn't kept his promise. Last month, he informed me that he didn't have enough vacation time to join me on this trip. I couldn't believe him. Our marriage was getting shakier and I needed some time with him, but once again, the job came before me. He didn't know that I had gone to an attorney to seek information about a divorce. We needed this trip to recapture something in our six-year-old marriage. Thoughts began to flood my mind about our marriage, my loneliness, my unexpressed hurt... the tears came down faster, I could now taste salty tears in my mouth, my body was jerking, and I turned my body toward the window and continued to cry.

I was born in Longview, Texas, on May 5, 1942. My mother decided to leave Texas after my birth and move to California with my two older brothers and sister. She wanted to find better employment and start out new, somewhere other than Texas. She arrived in San Francisco, California, with four children, in the summer of 1943, along with her sister, Elsie, and her sister's husband, Harvest. They found housing which had been converted into low income housing... in other words, in the ghetto. We all lived together in a two bedroom, one bath, living room and kitchen apartment. The apartment was too hot to sleep in during the summer, and in the winter, it was too cold because the small gas heater was not enough to keep the house warm.

During most of my childhood, I watched a great deal of television, especially the westerns and cartoons on Saturday morning. It was my main source of entertainment. Somewhere, around four years of age, my mother took me to the Golden Gate Theater in San Francisco to see a colored performer— Josephine Baker. I will never forget that moment in my life.

I remember her asking for children to come on stage and dance with her and I told my mother I wanted to go. My mother took me backstage and I walked on stage with Josephine Baker. I can still remember what she wore... a long, white, sequined gown with a slit up one side, revealing black fishnet stockings, and white high heel shoes. She had her hair in a beehive with curls cascading down one side of her head, thick false eyelashes (the kind that used to be on Koobie dolls in arcades), a false beauty mark (mole), beautiful white teeth surrounded by a smile, and beautiful, long nails painted red. Wow! I knew then I wanted to be a stage performer and a dancer. I thought she was the most beautiful colored woman I'd ever seen.

After I had danced on stage along with the other children, she gave us each a Josephine Baker doll. That day, I asked my mother if I could take dancing lessons. Later, this event lead me to see Lionel Hampton, a group named Red, Curly, and [the late] Will Masten Trio (Sammy Davis, Jr. and his uncles tap dancing). When I saw Sammy Davis, Jr. dance, I knew I wanted to learn how to tap dance. Later, I saw the Katherine Dunham Dancers, and I was sold on African-Haitian dancing. Finally, I saw a revue with Eartha Kitt, and I knew I wanted to be a performer. All of these people influenced me to take dance lessons until I was eighteen years of age.

However, somewhere along the way, my mother discouraged me from taking dancing serious because I was "too short and colored people couldn't really make a good living by dancing," and I should "put my energies into getting an education."

I always enjoyed school. My mother never had a problem getting me up to go to school in the morning... I loved school. When I was in kindergarten, a fellow classmate, Raymond Piggins, hit me over the head with a chair. This incident created a loss of hearing in my left hear and years of going to ear, nose, and throat clinics to try to restore my hearing. I used to get yelled at a great deal during my childhood until my mother realized I couldn't hear out of my left ear. Then she felt sorry over all of the punishment she had given me (she would spank me with a belt) because she thought I was a stubborn, unresponsive child.

School was a safe haven for me in many ways. I got attention, I was acknowledged, and I was appreciated in that environment. I enjoyed reading books, artwork, and playing with other children. In fact, I was selected in the fourth grade to go on a radio program to represent my fourth-grade class at Bret Harte Elementary School.

When I was nine years of age, life around me began to change. My uncle and aunt had moved out of our apartment in Double Rock and bought a house in the lower part of San Francisco's Bayview District. My older brother was an admired baseball player, my sister was an accomplished pianist, and my brother, four years older than me, was an honor student, athlete, and musician. Things were changing in our neighborhood, and my mother became protective of me. Young negro men were killing each other over a dime, a piece of clothing, a girlfriend, and my mother was afraid for us to go places without her acknowledgment. Young negro girls were becoming pregnant, and domestic violence was an every Friday and Saturday night occurrence.

Life was becoming more confusing for me. My mother worked as a domestic housekeeper to support us, and she was rarely at home because she was always taking care of someone else's house, and then coming home late to be with her children. I was left from the age of four through twelve years of age with my sister, brothers, or aunt and uncle to take care of me. I never was able to bond with my mother during these years. I really felt very much on my own, without much guidance from her. It was a source of despair for me during these years to have so many people telling me what to do and never really feeling I had done anything right, and being punished physically for not knowing how to do things to their satisfaction. I had no emotional support from my mother, nor anyone else during these years. I experienced childhood diseases, loss of hearing, curvature of the spine, and incest, without my family every knowing how I felt about these events. No one was concerned about my feelings—after all, their feelings were far more important than mine.

My sister got married at nineteen and my older brother at twenty-one, both in the year of 1953. This was another transition in our family. Now my mother was faced with her two older children leaving the nest, and her two younger children at home. My mother had a great deal of hope for, and expectations of, both of her older children becoming great achievers and having a better life than she had experienced. She was not pleased with their early marriages, but she was going to be supportive of them, and be available if they needed any help. This was a turning point for my life. As I see it, my mother discovered she had a fourth child... me. She now turned all of her disappointment and despair about my older siblings toward me and I became her emotional support.

I spent the next several years of my life being there emotionally for family members—mother, brothers, sister, aunts, uncles. I became the parent to my mother and without their knowledge, my brothers and sister as well. It was me my mother sought out to make decisions about money, or the personal sufferings and struggles of my sister and brothers. It was me she asked for advice about what she should or should not do for them. The role I was thrust into was burdensome, heavy, and filled with responsibility. What does a child of thirteen know about how to be a parent to her mother, her sister and her brothers? This was a time for me to enjoy my youth, but I was being deprived of my childhood with all of these responsibilities.

When I graduated from Portola Junior High School, I was an honor student who had held student-body office and received the American Legion Award for the most outstanding student in her class. I was excited about going to high school because I was finally going to attend a school where my sister and brothers had not attended. The pressure of following my brothers and sister's footsteps was coming to an end. I could finally be my own person with a level of academic achievement measured according to my own ability. I had selected Lowell High School as the school I wanted to attend because I wanted to go to college. At this time, my mother, my brother, and me had lived in a section named South Basin, and we were moving to the Potrero Hill housing projects.

After my first semester at Lowell High School, I wanted to transfer. I had always thought of myself as an open-minded person, but there were many Caucasian students at this school who needed an attitude adjustment. I was a member of the CSF (California Scholastic Federation), an honor students' group, and one of the things this group offered was a tutoring of certain subjects for other students who were having difficulty in earning passing grades. Many of the students came from wealthier sections of San Francisco (Sea Cliff, the Marina, Cow Hollow), and although their wealth didn't affect me, their attitudes did. I can remember tutoring Caucasian students whose parents could afford a private tutor, but who did not show up for scheduled appointments with me.

My English teacher, Mr. Englander, called me in his office and attempted to talk me out of making the transfer and to hang in there at Lowell. But I had a great many things happening in my household and the added pressure of classmates with attitudes was more than I could handle. I respected Mr. Englander for giving me such sound advice and caring about me as a student—his going the extra mile really meant a great deal to me.

I transferred to Galileo High School in the North Beach area and graduated in 1960 in the top 5 percent of my class, and earned a scholarship to attend college. It was at Galileo that I became aware of students from other ethnicities—Greek, Chinese, Japanese, Italian. Galileo was located near the Presidio, and Fort Mason and military housing was located across the street from the school. Attending Galileo High School was like attending a mini-United Nations enclave. It was a wonderful experience to meet students with other cultural backgrounds It was a beginning of my expanded interest in languages, cultures, and travel.

As a high school student, I had dreamed of going away to college, of being an exchange student and living in a foreign country. My experience of living in housing projects seemed so limiting and I wanted to see the world. During my last year of high school, my mother had fought for me to stay in school full-time and not to have to participate in a student/work program our social worker wanted me to work in. I really appreciated my mother's untiring efforts to challenge the social worker's efforts to force this upon me. As I look back, my mother absorbed and carried a great deal of degradation, humiliation and embarrassment as a single parent/head of the household during my childhood years, and the welfare system played a great part in this.

My mother is a very wise woman. She knew being on welfare was a temporary financial status and she wanted more for herself. My brother was attending college when I graduated from high school, and upon my graduation, welfare assistance ceased. My mother had to develop a way for us to survive. The cessation of welfare created a need for us to want more. So once again, we made another move to another housing project—Hunters Point. I was not happy with the move, but financially, we couldn't afford better housing, so we moved.

During the next two years, my mother became ill and could only work part-time. The burden of financial support fell upon me. I wanted to go away to college, but once again my dreams were deferred. I lost my financial assistance for college because I had to find employment to survive. I was angry because I had wanted my brothers and sister to help support my mother so I could go away to college. It never happened. I ended up working in the daytime and going to college in the evenings for approximately two years. I finally ended this scenario by dropping out of college. My grades were suffering from the work and the added responsibility of taking care of my mother.

My mother's health began to improve and I encouraged her to find employment at U.C. Medical Center in San Francisco. She was hired for a position in pediatrics. We both now had the same employer and we were planning to save money to buy a house. I was tired of living in housing projects and I wanted something better.

It took me twenty years working during the day and attending school at night to earn my B.S. degree in marketing. Along the way, I suffered seven years of sexual abuse (three of those years during high school) and five major surgeries.

Somewhere in the late seventies, my older brother was living in Los Angeles. I would visit him quite frequently, and during one of my weekend visits my sister-in-law asked me to read a book someone had given her. It was called *The Dynamic Laws of Prosperity* by Catherine Ponder. This book changed my life. It was the beginning of a transition point for me. I began to put into practice the things I read in the book and my life began to take on some new dimensions.

I was becoming frustrated with my lifestyle, and I wanted to take more control of my life. I decided to move out of the home my mother and I lived in and move to Oakland. I had lived with my mother for over thirty years and it was time to be on my own. Many people were surprised and shocked when I moved—especially my brothers and sister. It was an accepted belief that I would be living with my mother for the rest of my life. Again, no one knew how all of those years of responsibility had taken a toll on me personally. I needed my own life.

I left my job at U.C. Medical Center in 1964 and found employment at Crown Zellerbach Corporation (where I worked for twenty-one years). During these working years, my mother, my brothers, and my sister were still a major focus in my life. In 1979, I got married and my focus shifted to my husband. He had been married before and had two daughters from his previous marriage. I was on cloud nine when I got married and had expectations of creating a family. My expectations of having children by that marriage failed to happen along with other expectations about marriage. Looking back, I was more naive about marriage than I thought I was. The man I married was successful and a workaholic. I believe we both had a great deal of unfinished psychological garbage that we should have shed before marriage, and neither one of us knew it. Our marriage ended in divorce in 1987. The divorce was devastating to me—it was like a part of me died.

I first saw Roland J. Gilbert in 1985. He was attending Bible study classes at our church. I remember the first time I saw him because I thought he was arrogant—he was challenging the guest speaker on some point of scripture. My first thought was, what does he know about the subject? I didn't see Roland again until late 1986. I was attending a friend's Sunday school and he was there. His face seemed familiar, but I couldn't remember where I'd seen him. On the second visit to my friend's Sunday school class, I saw him in class again. It was on this day that I decided I wanted to be a Sunday school teacher.

The next Sunday I attended a training for all Sunday school teachers and much to my surprise, Roland was at the meeting. Roland was very personable and had a way of making others comfortable. Everyone in the class was concerned about our ability to become good teachers and make it through the eight-month training program. We decided to create a support group and we all exchanged phone numbers and began to hold weekly meetings. Over the next eight months, our group became closer, and we had a great deal of fun studying scripture, taking exams, and finally selecting an age group we wanted to teach.

During this time, Roland and I continued to grow in our understanding of God and his relationship to us, but it wasn't until 1988 that we both would attend a seminar that would change the course of our individual lives and our collective future. We attended a PSI (People Synergistically Involved) Seminar in South San Francisco, and it was here that our personal lives began to unravel. The seminar was a wake-up call in my life. The universe opened up and provided me with a new consciousness. The seminar was an experimental workshop based on the book, *The Dynamic Laws of Prosperity*.

The seminar allowed me to reflect back over my forty some years of life and realize everything that had happened to me was for a greater purpose—to allow me to give back and make a difference in the world. All of my suffering and pain was for my own good, to make me the person I am today. All of my life's experiences were my personal testimony of how suffering builds character. It is how I have accepted these sufferings and how I chose to use these sufferings in my life that has created my own uniqueness as a human being.

I don't believe my meeting Roland J. Gilbert was a coincidence. I don't believe my desire to make a difference in the lives of African American children is a coincidence. Roland and I share the same dream.

Somewhere along the way of my life, I remember saying to myself, "No child should have to experience the childhood that I experienced." My personal pain comes from never experiencing what it was, and is, to be a daughter and never experiencing what it was, and is, to be a sister to my brothers and sister, because I was cast into the role of a parent early in life. My other issues were abandonment, emotional abuse, psychological abuse and the loss of innocence.

My childhood experience created a unique human being who created her own individual defense mechanisms and coping techniques to survive. Every child needs to have safety and security—without this, children are wounded very early and become victims to circumstances and events. I believe my advocacy for the child has been there all along. Simba is the outgrowth of my advocacy for the child.

On March 30, 1990, I married Roland J. Gilbert. It is a union of love and a joint commitment to the vision of Simba. In the initial stages of our marriage, Roland created the sixty-six-hour Simba leadership seminar for African American men. But we knew that both men and women needed to be whole in order to create a new generation of African American children.

On July 7, 1993, we had our first Simba women's leadership seminar with twelve participants. Two weeks later, we had our second seminar with seven participants. My biggest challenge for the Simba women's seminar was having my husband as a part of the seminar. The women were expecting me as the sole instructor, and they were quite surprised to find Roland present during their training.

Both seminars have provided me with validation of my own personal belief about African American women—they fear vulnerability. We have been defined and programmed to believe that we have to be strong. However, it is the experience of vulnerability that allows us to become aware of our weaknesses and provides us with an opportunity to become more alive and healthier human beings.

The seminars have also provided us with knowledge of our men—how brothers, fathers, uncles, etc. color our knowledge of men and how they give women a blueprint of what men are all about. Black women's major issues are absentee fathers and emotionally shut-down men. This is not surprising to me because my personal background reflects the same things—an absent father, an intelligent brother who sought drugs for emotional control, an intellectual brother who sought a sense of family through several marriages, and a workaholic ex-husband who needed to be loved and showed love the same way my father and brothers did, with no emotional involvement, but merely a physical presence.

I have come to realize that we are doing the best we know how based upon our life experiences, and what we have had modeled to us by other human beings. I have forgiven all the people who have done things to me that have created pain and suffering for me. And in return, I continue to forgive myself for all the things I may have done to others who received pain from my behavior. For it is truly in forgiving that you give and receive love. Forgiving is not for the other person, but it is for the forgiver. It allows you to free yourself of the emotional buy-in that keeps you connected to that person.

The support system that black women have is really supporting the very things that need to be changed. They already know that they're strong and that they gotta do it by themselves, but the hardest thing for black women is asking for help. Many of us just don't know how to do it. Especially when it comes to black men.

Boys are loved. Girls are raised. As black women, we don't know where love comes from. We know that we're supposed to love and nurture, but we don't know where love comes from. So somewhere in that process, women begin to ask, "How can we just be loved? How can we be vulnerable?" Women feel that they have to earn love, men don't.

Black women as a whole fit into that Eurocentric view more so than black men. We were the ones who were able to make that bridge between white culture and the black culture. Black men weren't going to do it. They refused to do it. Black women are really thrust into being too responsible and too mature too early, to compensate for the absence of the black male or because of the perception that the black male will not be there for them, so they need to be prepared.

Many sisters have "attitudes" today because they were passed down to them from their mothers and grandmothers. Their resentment of black men and particularly towards their place in American society, comes largely from slavery. Black women have been subjected to having to be in a position to nurture and be responsible for a lot of stuff. She didn't have anyone to clean her house, take care of her kids, to take care of her, honor, and cherish her. She took on a persona of a much more masculine role. It wasn't that the black man couldn't help, it was that he was not allowed to help. In many cases, if he did, the consequences would be death or complete separation from his family.

So the bottom line was that the black woman could not count on her man to be there for her in many ways. The black woman was the mammy. She was responsible for the house, the mistress, the kids, her family, her man, everything. Many people don't see that the black man was there with his family, even against all of the things slavery did to separate them. The black man and the black woman were not dysfunctional, they were forced into a dysfunctional system. A system where the white man made his wife the symbol of perfect beauty and put her on a pedestal. Then he made the black woman the care-taker. That was the white man's version of family, and it was dysfunctional. That was the white man's way of having a family, by exploiting the black family.

One hundred and thirty years after slavery, many of those programs are still in place. The biggest program for black women is the one that says, "I don't need nobody. I can do it all myself." So the Simba Women's leadership seminar helps sisters take a deep look at themselves and helps them to understand they don't have to be responsible for everything—that they can get help, even from African American men. My Simba experience has taught me that we can all make a difference everyday, by standing on our rock, and being a leader of ourselves.

We, as black women, have had many traditions passed down to us from our mothers, their mothers, and their mother's mothers. These traditions, we have just accepted as the only way to be an African American woman. To question whether there is another way to experience black womanhood is not a matter of blaming our mothers but rather recognizing that these traditions may be ineffective in today's society—and if they are, Why do we continue to adhere to them?

The women that have chosen to attend the Leadership workshop, learn to shed their emotional and psychological responsibilities. In their own words, let them tell you about their experiences:

Rolandra Ragsdale, 30, Counselor
My first day at the seminar was very helpful. I liked the rules because for me, I work better with rules. And it taught me structure—I had to do certain things every night. Since my brother Keith was in it, I kinda was aware of some things already. Like I know you're supposed to check on your sisters, you know , things like that.

On Thursday, we had to tell stories about our moms. We had divided into different groups, and on one side of the room, in one group, you talked about your father. Then you switched and went to the other side and talked about your mother. And I could barely get it out without crying.

I had a whole bunch of hurt feelings, things I really need to talk about, and I didn't know how. I used to always talk about my mom, but I always used to laugh about it—you know, I think that was just a cover-up. At first Roland started off asking questions about my relationships with men, but I don't think that was really my big issue. But then the final picture was my mother. She committed suicide when I was a teenager, and she made me give her the matches to set the room on fire—and also, about her abuse, and her being abusive, and me being scared of her and my shame, and me carrying the guilt for years for giving her the matches—things like that. Basically, I just think I needed to get it out. I thought I had dealt with the issue at one time. I used to be on cocaine, and I when I went into a rehab center, I kind of grieved over feeling guilty over giving my mother the matches. But this time it was different. Just to be able to say stuff out loud helped a lot.

It was kind of hard for me to realize that a man can't make you happy. You know, for years and years I looked to men to make me happy, give me joy, things like that. But I learned that I couldn't really get that from men. That I have to get them for myself and they can't give me none of that. So it's like now I'm going through the change, and it's kind of deep for me to realize that they can't give me that, and it's like what were they supposed to give me, you know.

So I'm working on that a little bit, and to just tell them what I want and things like that, so after the seminar I had a lot of heavy things on my mind. I think I learned stuff from my mother, cause she always had boyfriends, and she was the type that was always doing things for them. She looked after the men first. Yeah, that's where it started, I learned not to say no to my mate. A pleaser, you know—I'm supposed to cook and things like that.

I know my Chapter is going to be a dynamite Chapter. I never did like women, so at first this was a new experience for me, to be able to call them and say I love you and get with them and do things with them. In the past, I didn't have no time for women. Probably 'cause I didn't trust them. But these women, I got a bond.

Naponisha Sivad, 27, Writer

At first I felt violated, and I resented the whole process. Roland went on and on about my agreement. My biggest thing was that someone could agree to do something, but they might not understand exactly. One person could say one thing, and we could all have a different understanding of what was said. Then he asked me if I had asked for any clarity. And I said "no," because at the time, everything seemed clear. He asked me where else in my life was I assuming that everything was clear and then not asking for more information. I realized that I was doing that a lot.

We had a lot of resistance towards Roland. I think a lot of it was because we didn't want to share in front of a man. Even before the seminar, I knew I had some respect issues towards men. Most of the men in my family are like mama's boys. They pretty much have been handicapped by their parents, by their mother. Most of them were raised in single-family homes. And most of them still depend on their moms, even though they are adults. I've never been able to really rely on men for anything. If anything, I've had to bail them out a lot. I come from a single-parent family, and since I never saw a mother and father, I didn't assume that I was going to have that reality. So everything I did, I did with the possibility that I would be alone. Part of the reason I went to law school was because, whatever it was, I wanted to be able to afford to have children with or without a man. The whole thing was that "he may be there in the beginning but he may not be there throughout."

I had a pretty dramatic childhood as far as violence and stuff. So what I would do was replicate that. I would find a man who either was abusive or curse at me or be physical, or just be emotionally unavailable. I attracted those kind of men. If there was a big party, and there was one quiet man who was sitting in the corner, kind of handsome, and had a nice haircut—if he was somebody that I could fix up, then I knew there was a problem before I even approached him. But I did it anyway. Another thing is, I would choose short-term relationships because I really feared the intimacy of committed, long-term relationships. My mother passed when I was fourteen and I just feared becoming emotionally attached to somebody that way. I had emotional needs, and I would meet them for a minute, and then break up.

I realized that I have a lot of hurt. I also realized that I have to approve of myself for myself. I was always seeking approval from others. I can love myself and love other people too. When I went through Simba, I realized that I don't have to do anything that I don't want to do. It was easy after I realized that I didn't have to be right. Basically, I've always lived with fear. Now, I don't fear things like I did before the seminar. If fear comes up, I recognize it as fear and I don't give it as much power.

My parents divorced when I was two years old. My father didn't live with me. When I was eleven, he was incarcerated, and he was incarcerated for eleven years. So when he got out, it was kind of late for him to be a father—as far as I was concerned. I really didn't see him like that anyway. I saw him as sort of an uncle. I dealt with my father more like a child in a way, 'cause he's always been so irresponsible. I keep him at a distance. I don't really rely on him, not even emotionally. The biggest thing I learned about black men growing up was "a nigga ain't shit." I don't feel that way now, but that was my sentiment.

I think Simba can empower black men. Most of the men I encountered prior to Simba talked about the white man or somebody doing something to them. They were really in the victim role, and it didn't allow them any time to really work on themselves. When I met Chris it was different. I wasn't responsible for whether he was happy or sad. I was used to trying to make everybody happy and be pleasing. And when I didn't have to do that, I was thrilled. The biggest part for men is taking responsibility for themselves and also their feelings, because this society doesn't promote a man feeling anything. For black men, the only acceptable feeling is anger and violence. I learned that women don't have to take care of them.

I learned that its OK to feel vulnerability. Where as before my attitude was—there was no way that I can rely on a man for anything. Before my awareness in Simba, in a way, I didn't feel like I really experienced life. I was just existing, surviving. Simba has been a "10" experience for me.

Chapter 13

1993

Robert and I had just left the KTVU television station doing an interview together on their morning news show called "Mornings On 2." We were on our way to breakfast, and Robert was quietly sitting next to me in the car as we drove to the restaurant. He broke my driver's hypnotic trance and startled me back into the present with, "I am so proud of myself. I want you to know that I really like me and I have really learned that honesty is the best policy." I asked him what he meant by that.

He said that he and four other boys who weren't in Simba were playing, and one of the boys had a can of spray paint. They sprayed some on the sidewalk and so did he. Then one of them sprayed a parked car. They asked Robert to spray a car too and he said no. Somebody called the police and the boy's mother who sprayed the car got them into the house and asked them what happened. Well, Robert told her what had happened but the mother's son denied it. He lied about it. But she believed the other boys.

"I told the other boys not to feel bad about telling the truth to his mom because it was best for him and all of us."

Well, the boy who painted the car agreed to work for the owner of the car every week until it was paid for. Robert decided to talk to his friend and ask him who he was mad at. The friend tried to use one of the other boys as his excuse for what he did. But Robert told him that he had to take responsibility for his own actions.

"I told him that he was OK , but what he did was not. And then I asked him if he learned a lesson, and he said, 'to leave other peoples stuff alone and not to mess with spray paint again.'" Robert talked to his friend about how he felt about the other boys having told on him, and helped him work through his anger and resolve his feelings and told him to go directly to the other boys and talk to them about everything.

Robert then asked the boy to please apologize to his mom for lying to her, to let her know that he will never do that again, and to put aside all his anger and stop crying and whining.

"And I asked him if he wanted me to stay with him because I was already late getting home. It was 8:45 p.m. and I was due home by 8:30 p.m. But I said that this was more important and told him not to be responsible for my choosing to stay. I was 'off purpose' because I could have called home and I didn't, or I could've run home and come back, but I didn't. So he asked me to stay while he talked to his mom.

"We talked together about this a couple times later. The car was fixed OK, and he didn't get a whipping, but he is on punishment. I was very proud of myself. And I came home and told my grandma I was proud of the way I handled it. And I am going to start dealing with hanging around with the wrong crowd, when I have a choice, when I know I could stay away from that crowd. But it worked out good and that's my story."

And I said, "I am very proud of you, too, Robert."

Since being in Simba, Robert has learned new ways of dealing with problems. Most importantly, he has learned that *he* is not his behavior, that he will make mistakes and when he does, he needs to take responsibility for his actions, learn from them, forgive himself and move forward. But when I heard how he was teaching this to other children, I knew he had become what I and his other Simba leaders had become—a man who takes responsibility for how he thinks, feels, and acts. I saw a bright future for Simba and our people.

Robert's story shows some of the tools our Simba leaders give to our boys and girls. These are the tools our children need first, to know how to be both an emotional human being and yet meet life's challenges head on. All human beings on earth need these tools. Dr. Jawanza Kunjufu alludes to this in his wonderful, three-volume book set, *Countering The Conspiracy To Destroy Black Boys*, which is required reading for all Simba leaders. Our children also need to understand their unique history and culture. This is an important part of our one-year

Rites-of-Passage component, in which we use Dr. Nathan Hare's book, *Bringing The Black Boy To Manhood*.

Dr. Jawanza Kunjufu
Renowned educator, author, lecturer, and president of African American Images, a communication company based in Chicago, Illinois, Dr. Kunjufu has been a guest on "The Oprah Winfrey Show," "Tony Brown's Journal," and Black Entertainment Television.

Q. What are some of the biggest problems facing African American men?

A. Ninety-five percent of the brothers who are in jail right now have five things in common: They can't read beyond a sixth-grade reading level, they don't have a high school diploma, they weren't given one course in African American history and culture, they were on street corners between 10:00 at night and 3:00 in the morning, and they didn't go to Sunday school. Let me also add two other major factors. One would be the lack of a black, male role-model. Sixty-two percent of black children don't have their fathers at home. The second one would be the change in the economy. In 1920, 90 percent of our youth had their fathers at home. In 1960, 80 percent had them at home. But in 1993, only 38 percent have their fathers at home. I believe that's directly related to the economy in that the economy shifted from agriculture to industrialism to the service sector. We were brought to this country to work. There was an economic need for black men to be here. That economic need no longer exists. So America has a problem with a people they no longer need. What we have to do as an African people is to ask ourselves, what are we going to do for ourselves in terms of economic development and entrepreneurship?

Q. Can you explain your "conspiracy theory," from your book *The Conspiracy to Destroy Black Boys*?

A. The conspiracy theory is based on the concept of white male supremacy. If you live in a world controlled by white men, and we do—a world where all forty-two presidents have been white men, where a white boy with a high school diploma makes more money than anyone else in America with a college degree—then it's obvious that the greatest threat to white men does not come from women, but come from other men. The Fortune 500, the Tri-Lateral Commission, and the Senate are all controlled by white men.

Q. In the book, you talk about the "Fourth Grade Failure Syndrome" and how black boys psychologically begin to drop out. What do you think parents can do to stop that? And do you feel that they contribute to that negatively?

A. As the age increases, parental involvement decreases. Now that's what parents do incorrectly. They give less time to their children as they become older, when in reality they should give more. The solution, then, is to reverse that. When the age increases, you should increase the amount of involvement. Because unfortunately, as the age increases, peer pressure, media, and the influence of rap—the major three competitors for our children— become greater. As a result, parental involvement decreases. Another issue is that some mothers are raising their daughters and loving their sons. They have double standards for their sons and daughters. They teach their daughters how to cook, sew, and clean, but not their sons. They make their daughters study, come in early, and go to church, but not their sons.

Q. What are some of the biggest failures of the educational system toward African American boys?

A. Eighty-five percent of the African American children who are placed into Special Ed. are male. Thirty-seven percent of the students suspended in public schools are African American males.

American schools have designed a female classroom with large numbers of male students, and black males suffer more than any other group. So the problem starts with a black boy's not having a father at home. Then it gets compounded in a female-designed classroom, so black boys are then not doing as well academically.

Then we have an economy that is now based on computer skills, critical thinking skills, and literacy skills, and black men suffer from this bias. So it makes it very difficult. The overall concept of "tracking"—that's where you divide children based on ability— means that, unfortunately, most black males are placed in the lowest reading group or the lowest achievement group available. The other problem is that of low expectations. There's a direct relationship between expectations and academic achievement. Many schools lower their expectations for African American, male students.

Last, but not least, we make up 17 percent of the students in public schools, but only 8 percent of the teachers, nationwide. And African American *males* comprise only 1.2 percent of teachers.

Q. So a cycle has evolved in the black community. If the child wasn't raised right, then as a man, he won't know how to raise his son. Where do you think this cycle started and what can be done to stop it?

A. I think it would have to stop with teenage pregnancy. African American females lead the world in teen pregnancy. Seven out of ten of our children are born out of wedlock, and they are primarily being born to children under nineteen years of age. A lot of studies point out that we had babies at young ages even twenty to forty years ago. But marriage also accompanied that fact. That's not happening now. So the morality piece is one factor, but the economic issue is the major one.

In terms of where this problem starts, we have a fourteen-year-old girl giving birth to a young boy, with no father available. And because these mothers are insecure and immature, they are not comfortable with teachers and older adults chastising their children. So we have a fourteen- or fifteen-year-old child raising a child by herself—that's not going to work. Number two, the extended family is not there. It used to be that the parents' neighbors on the block also helped rear children, and today that's not taking place. So when that happens, it becomes a case of the gangs versus rites-of-passage programs for our youth. And right now the gangs are winning. The gangs work twenty-four hours a day, seven days a week, and we don't have enough rites-of-passage programs in as many places as we need them. And wherever they are, they only work for two hours, one day a week.

Q. What significance do rites-of-passage programs have for African American boys?

A. There are nine areas we work on: spirituality, history, economics, politics, career development, community involvement, family responsibility, physical development, and the Nguzo Saba. Those are nine very important areas of development. They define manhood. However, the gang's definition of manhood is how many women you have, how many babies you make, how much reefer you can smoke, how many people you've killed, or if you've gone to jail and come out unrehabilitated.

Q. In your area, are there any Simba programs working with boys?
A. There are about eight of them. Each program may have twenty boys each, so that's 160 boys. But the gangs could have 100,000. And gang members spend more time with each other. It's hard to get men to consistently come out every Saturday from ten to twelve. And the gangs create a family for the boys.
   A lot of boys can't even imagine what it's like to live in a real household. After they've been on the streets all day and come home hungry and gone to the refrigerator and found there's nothing there, and their mama is on the phone talking to her girlfriend and turns to the boy and says, "What the hell did you come home for?" So the boy is angry.
   A lot of our children have not been hugged, have not been loved, have not been nurtured, and the gangs have provided some of that.

Q. What, in your opinion, is the ghetto solution?
A. Well, I don't know if I can answer that. I would recommend my latest book called *Hip Hop vs. MAAT*. There's an exercise called the Killing Exercise and the Malcolm X Classroom that addresses a ghetto solution.

Dr. Nathan Hare
Scholar, author, and activist, Dr. Hare (along with his wife, Dr. Julia Hare) has written several books, including Bringing the Black boy to Manhood: The Passage. *He was the founding publisher of* The Black Scholar *magazine and he has published dozens of articles in* Ebony, Newsweek, Black World, USA Today, *and* The Times of London, *to name a few. Dr. Hare holds two Ph.D.'s (in clinical*

psychology and sociology) and, with his wife, oversees the Black Think Tank in San Francisco, CA.

Q. Please discuss some of the major points of your book, *Bringing the Black boy to Manhood.*

A. We had been concerned that the black boy does not get told that he is a man. So he experiences an extended adolescence. He could get up to fifty years old before he really begins to feel like he's a man. I thought that we should go back and study some of our African traditions from the past and go back and take the best and leave the rest. We were trying to make the point that the black male doesn't have any psycho-biological signal of manhood. So a sense of responsibility is never developed.

Q. How did the book address the psycho-social needs of the boys?

A. Black people especially suffer from what psychologists call "Locus of Control." [This needs further clarification; that their problem is always yielding to an external locus of control.] This means they don't have the experience of being able to control their destiny or the outside world, so they focus on themselves. But they externalize all the blame and responsibility, putting it out there, so they don't deal with their own lives. We had been interested in Africa long before it was popular to be so, but we didn't see it as the panacea so many people now do.

Q. In your research of rites-of-passage training in traditional Africa, was there any kind of training that the men went through?

A. I don't recall any. I know that most men in Africa had already had preparation for manhood.

Q. Without a rites-of-passage, when and how do African American men know that they're men, and what's the psychological fallout of that?

A. Well, it becomes a long, drawn-out affair. It affects their dealings with their mates, their children, the occupational world, power relations, the white man, everything. You can join the army at eighteen, get rank at twenty-one, and get married, and then people start calling you a man. But these are all the rules according to white society. Du Bois' double-lens theory talked about the dilemma. We have to look at the world through two lenses—one black, one white.

You know you're a man, but you don't get a complete validation of that from society. So the most frequent thing a black man is likely to do is to become very good at athletics, entertainment, and so on, but these are all adolescent things.

In the seventies, even the black man's compensatory masculinity and his psychological masculinity were denigrated by society, which called it "macho." And it was sexism to be macho. Then, in the eighties, they turned it around and said that the black man had been robbed of all of the social meaning of his masculinity. Then they wanted to analyze his psyche. What we really need to do is change his social environment.

The rites-of-passage becomes a quasi-social means of getting the black male on the road to masculinity. We have to change things on a social level. Many black intellectuals and leaders don't address these things, even in private. What they do is try to get accepted into whatever models the white liberal makes. This is why we're not properly dealing with the black man's problem; we let them deal with it psychologically. We take a sociological problem, something that the world or the environment has made, and instead of dealing with that, we deal with the psyche of the individual.

Q. What, in your opinion, is the ghetto solution?

A. Well, there are so many. It's been said that it takes as many different kinds of people to find solutions as it takes to make the world. One of the problems is we've started looking for solutions before we've understood the problem. Part of it is many of us look around and use white solutions, using the same thing that causes the problem to deal with it. So the main solution to the problem of the black child in the ghetto is for them to get back control over their socialization, of which a rites-of-passage is only one aspect. The problem of socialization is the biggest part of the problem.

The real problem of the black race is their inability to gain psychological, cognitive, effective independence from the white world. That is, white people pretend that black people are white with black-face and black people think that they are essentially whites with black-face. Their inability to think differently from the white race's agenda is a big one.

Roland Gilbert, Founder of Simba, Inc.

I visited a Simba Leadership Training Seminar the other day. As founder of the program and creator of the training seminar this was a very special event for me. I was not needed. Christopher Billups and Keith Ragsdale were establishing their first Simba Chapter completely on their own. I thought about the other instructors who have completed training and will soon be on their own. And I also thought about the women completing training. some of whom are already demanding a date to be trained as instructors.

My heart is full. My dream is coming true. I designed Simba to help adults and children become their own leaders. Leaders of themselves. I trained the instructors to do the same. Yet as I watched, I was still torn between holding on and letting go, between being the leader and letting others lead.

You see, each training seminar is the story of my life and it is the giving of my life to others. All human beings share this common cycle of life: pain, discovery, truth, choice, letting go, receiving, healing, joy and growth. Both seeing these young men doing their own sharing and giving their lives to others and with their request to me to teach them to become trainers of instructors, I knew the cycle had begun and Simba's future was assured.

CHILDREN LEARN WHAT THEY LIVE
by Dorothy Law Nolte

If a child lives with criticism,
  He learns to condemn.

If a child lives with hostility,
  He learns to fight.

If a child lives with ridicule,
  He learns to be shy.

If a child lives with shame,
  He learns to feel guilty.

If a child lives with tolerance,
  He learns to be patient.

If a child lives with encouragement,
  He learns confidence.

If a child lives with praise,
  He learns to appreciate.

If a child lives with fairness,
  He learns justice.

If a child lives with security,
  He learns to have faith.

If a child lives with approval,
  He learns to like himself.

If a child lives with acceptance and friendship,
  He learns to find love in the world.

Chapter 14

The Solution

The only true and lasting ghetto solution is for the people to take full responsibility for how they think, feel, and act towards themselves, others, their circumstances and their environment. The problem is how to teach them to do that. The solution is Simba, Inc.

According to the United States Bureau of the Census, in 1989, there were 9,305,000 African Americans and 20,788,000 white Americans living below poverty level. So tell me, where are the white ghettos? In any city you go to, anybody can tell you where the black ghetto is located. You see, there are poor white communities with poor housing, inferior city services, unemployment, and so on, but we don't call them ghettos. And the people who live there don't call the area a ghetto, they don't see themselves as living in a ghetto, and they don't act like they live in a ghetto. The ghetto is a state of mind and spirit within people. It is not buildings and streets.

The obvious need for Head Start programs, better schools, improved healthcare services, adequate housing, basic nutrition, good-paying jobs, affordable child-care services, and effective and friendly police, fire, street repair and other city-services personnel should not be in question anywhere in America. In the ghetto, unfortunately, they are.

Yes, our people in the ghetto face racism, violence, death, drugs, crime, disease, poor schools and healthcare services, and inadequate nutrition and housing. And I say to our people living in the ghetto, you are right when you say these are obstacles in your life. Being right about this, however, and having a quarter will not buy you a cup of coffee. And if you are waiting for white people to apologize or for the government to save you, forget it. It has not happened in four hundred years, so what makes you think it ever will? *You* must be willing to make a difference, to go for the things you want from life. Don't just sit around being right and waiting for other people to make your life better. You have the power to create your future, independent of politics, the economy, your circumstances, or your environment.

To our people in the ghetto, I say that your real problem is that you don't know how to *be* different in order to *get* different results in your life. You are doing the best you can with what you know how to do. No one can do more than they know how to do. Doing demonstrates knowing. There are basically two different kinds of people—those who don't know and those who won't know. This is a call to action for all who don't know. This is a call to action to regain your power and create your future independent of your past and regardless of your current circumstances. If you want to learn how to do this, join with us in Simba and we will teach you. The choice is yours.

It is crucial that all people, and particularly white people, understand what happened to black people in America and around the world. No other race of people on the planet has ever been treated as black Africans were. Africans were purposely dehumanized as a marketing strategy for the slave trade, in America, and around the world. The U.S. government and the tobacco, cotton, general agriculture, gold, rum, brandy, spice and other industries had to sell slavery to the American people.

Racism had very little to do with it in the beginning, it was just business. In fact, indentured, white servants were tried for a while, but that didn't work too well because they would run away and were able to blend into a new community. Ah, but these *black* Africans were easily identifiable. But the real problem was how to sell this to the white-American people. Here was a group of predominantly white-skinned, straight-haired people from many different European countries that was trying to form a new country on the basis of freedom and individual human rights. These people had fought and died to get rid of dictators and oppressive governments. They wrote the Bill of Rights and the Declaration of Independence, both of which spoke about freedom and rights of individuals. At that point in history, it was truly revolutionary to speak of, or believe in, equal rights for all people.

So how was government and industry going to sell the

enslavement of people to this visionary citizenry? How were they going to get them to become oppressors, or at the very least, to condone oppression?—With the "big lie!"—They conspired to sell the white, American, freedom-loving people the idea that black Africans were not actually people. That they were a sub-human species that needed to be enslaved for their own good. That these people had no culture or history, and were savages running around like wild, godless animals.

This marketing strategy was so well presented that African Americans were voted into the U.S. Constitution as three-fifths of a person. This perception was also sold to citizens of other countries around the world by their governments, who had industries that depended upon the slave trade from Africa. Therefore, it was absolutely mandatory for them—America, and all the other countries involved—to destroy anything that supported the notion that black African people were intelligent human beings with a culture and morals, values, society, and a history.

The black-African people's history and culture were systematically and purposefully altered or destroyed by the major countries of the world so that their citizens would accept the enslavement of a "sub-human" species. This worldwide conspiracy and systematic destruction and falsification of a people's history has not been done to any other racial group on earth. Africa was not only raped and pillaged of its people and resources, but also of its history and culture so that the slave trade, the "big lie," could be perpetrated. They did an excellent job, one that has had a multi-generational effect on both white and black Americans. The insidious nature of this imagery is seen today in our ghettos and in many of the policies and programs designed to help ghetto people.

In programs , this multi-generational imagery is evident in the assumptions the programs are founded upon. Two major assumptions that we see played out are "those people" are basically defective and need someone to fix them, and "if we could just give 'those people' something—like jobs, housing, better leadership, or a number of other things—then they would be better people and would act better."

Both of these support the image that the segment of African American people residing in our ghettos is incapable of making good choices, taking charge of their lives and asking for the help that they need. This mindset assumes that African Americans can't think for themselves and they need an outside agency or organization to tell them what to do. Sound familiar? The "big lie."

We have an entire industry of modern-day missionaries, both government and private sector, that is reinforcing the image that ghetto people are incompetent individually and incapable collectively of working together to create a better future. How demeaning and destructive! So we continue to spend hundreds of millions of dollars on agencies and programs telling our people what to think, what kind of job to get, and what they are capable of doing and becoming. We must stop this. And let us begin to spend money on programs like Simba that teach people about the greatness within them and how to think in ways that empower them, rather than in ways that limit them—that teach people how to find the resources they need and produce the results they want. Thus our own belief as a country in the "big lie" is shown in the way our public policies, programs, and budgets are designed to do for people rather than help people do for themselves.

A major flaw in this strategy can be seen in the budget deficits at all levels of government—federal, state, county, and city. These budgetary problems are aggravated because we continue to deal with social issues through intervention after the problems arise. We have set up entire industries, both public and private, to deal with intervention. Instead, we must concentrate on prevention. We must teach people how to take responsibility for how they think, feel, and act. We must teach people how to get the results they want in their lives and give them the dignity and responsibility to be able to make good choices.

We cannot continue to legislate and pay for the results of other peoples' bad choices. We cannot afford it. As a country we are going broke, and our service systems are in overload and collapse. It is also a disservice and a degradation to the people we do it to.

Violence, crime, poverty, drug abuse, and murder can be totally eliminated by people making different choices. These choices are made as a result of how individuals see themselves and others, and how they think, feel, and act towards themselves and others. If all of the ghetto crime, violence, drug abuse, and murder was directed towards white Americans by black Americans, then I might say that it was a group of people defending themselves or attacking an oppressor. But this is not the case.

Instead, the vast majority of all of these acts are perpetrated by African Americans against African Americans. Clearly, to me, this is a multi-generational result of the excellent marketing job done on the image of African Americans—that black Americans who commit these crimes against their brothers have themselves bought the "big lie." When we are willing to see the truth, that the vast majority of our ghetto woes are done to us, by us, then we can move forward. Until we admit this, we will go on blaming white people and looking for them, or others outside of ourselves, to fix us and solve our problems. And the statistics will continue to get worse.

Someone once said, "You can't leave Chicago until you have arrived there." When we finally arrive at the realization that we are killing ourselves by our own choices, then we will be able to leave there by asking the all-important question: How can I learn to overcome my negative, self-destructive programming and make better choices for myself and my community? We also need to ask other important questions, like how can I learn to create better health, wealth, relationships, and self-expression for myself and my community? Simba teaches adults and children how to do this.

Our people in the ghetto have not been taught to be masters of themselves. They have been taught that others are their masters. That others have and they have not. And in order for them to have, they must get it from others. They have not been taught to create what they want. The ghetto solution is to get young people before their ghetto programming is fixed in place and virtually unchangeable and raise a generation of these young people. Give them a group of positive adults who themselves have, and are continuing to, overcome their own negative ghetto programming and other forms of negative slavery-time thinking patterns and let them teach the children— adults who will hold the children accountable for their choices and be responsible to them without being responsible for them. This is the only true and lasting ghetto solution.

Some of our political and community leaders believe that the reasons for our ghetto problems are guns, crack cocaine, and lack of jobs. The real problem is the way our people have learned to respond to these things, not the things themselves. We must stop our shortsightedness and blend into our quick fixes of external circumstances the long-term resolution of changing peoples lives internally. There is an old Chinese proverb that says, "If you want to think a year ahead, plant a seed; if you want to think ten years ahead, plant a tree; but if you want to think a hundred years ahead, educate the people."

We must begin to raise generations of children who will not choose violence, who will not choose crime, who will not choose drugs, who will not choose poverty, and who will not blame others and choose to be victims of their circumstances. We must raise children who will be who they choose to be, do what they choose to do, and have what they choose to have, just like many of their African ancestors before them. We must raise children who know that there is only one race on the planet Earth—the human race—and that they are spiritual beings living a human experience. Because of this, all the power they need is within them.

Presently, we would rather fund an agency that provides services to the ghetto community than to fund the training of the community to do it for itself. You can always tell what a person's true intentions are by how they spend their time and money. The same is true of governments, institutions, corporations, and nonprofit organizations.

One of the major problems we encounter in funding Simba chapters is that the prospective funders want to give to an organization with all the traditional trappings—budgets, overheads, financial statements, etc. Well, what we do in Simba has virtually no budget and no overhead. The only thing that we need funding for is the initial training of the community people. Then they take it from there, they raise their own children, with no further moneys required.

This they find hard to believe because of the popular misconception that African American men and women don't want to raise their own community's children. This misconception is also held by some black people, who more specifically believe that African American men don't want to help raise their children. This is just not true. It is not the issue at all. They just don't know how. When they do know how, they respond.

Some Simba leaders, on their own initiative, went out to recruit volunteers and came back with 934 African Americans who had registered for a Simba orientation to become Simba leaders. That's 592 men and 342 women. So don't tell me that African American men and women don't want to help ghetto children become effective, functioning adults.

As Americans, we know what results we wish to achieve in our society, we just don't know how. Well, Simba is the how. Simba is the vehicle for teaching our ghetto men and women how to raise our ghetto children and also how to improve their own lives. Simba is the answer to how we can make it work. Unfortunately, it will take a fundamental change in many people's thinking in order for this program to be accepted and supported.

A large California foundation received a letter of intent from us on violence prevention. Of the more than three hundred letters they received, sixty-eight were selected to submit full proposals. Simba was one of the sixty-eight selected. Eighteen grants were awarded. Simba was not one of the grantees. Those chosen were recognized organizations with lots of overhead and staff, that had been working in the community for years, providing services to the community rather than teaching the community to do things for themselves. As a result, when that funding ends, those services will stop.

It has not dawned on these funding institutions yet that people who have worked in the community for twenty years, doing the best they know how to do, have not come up with the solutions to deter the violence or to solve the ghetto's problems. But these funders continue to go the same route, to continue financing these established programs, and so the problems keep getting worse.

This does not mean these organizations are totally ineffective at what they do or that they are not providing a needed and worthwhile service; it just means that they do not know how to *solve* the problem. We need a new direction. While we are providing needed services to the community, we must simultaneously teach people how to create their own lives. Simba is a new idea whose time has come.

Our organization wants to go in and fix the problem. There is nothing inherently wrong with the people. What is wrong is how they have learned to think about themselves, their circumstances, and their environment. People *can* learn to think differently. We do it in Simba all the time. And it works. The attitude that there is something wrong with the people and we must fix them, is nothing more than the "big lie" that is part of black- and white-people's belief systems today. Traditional service providers end up behaving like benevolent "Masters," providing for those poor, incompetent people who are incapable of learning to do it for themselves. Sound familiar?

A white congressman at a bay area community conference said, "Poor people are poor because they don't have money." That white congressman doesn't understand the effect of his belief system. To say the poor are poor because they don't have money—is to disempower them. It tells them that if they can't get a job, which most ghetto residents can't, then the only way they can stop being poor is for someone to give them some money or to take it from someone who has it. In either case, their power is in someone else's hands and not their own. Someone else has their power, so they are just victims and powerless. This is a great example of the "Master mentality" handed down from slavery. This unquestioned programming of many white people contributes to the continuing disempowerment of ghetto people.

If you have this belief system, then ask yourself these questions:

1. Do we have enough money to give poor people so that they won't be poor?—Answer: No!

2. Will government and industry provide good jobs with good wages and good potential for advancement to all ghetto residents?—Answer: No!

3. Since we can't end poverty, what can we do?—Their answer: Let's spend some money on a few programs and help a few of them.

Isn't this what we see happening in America? There is no national, state, county, and city coordinated set of goals and strategic plans to eliminate poverty, violence, crime, and drug addiction. Why? Because our national, state, county, and city leaders do not believe we can. And they are right. We can't, the "Master" can't. But the people, with our help, can. Our governments spend their time and money on intervention, not prevention. We must do BOTH.

It is crucial that each one of us ask ourselves: What is it

about my belief systems that supports poverty, violence, crime and drug abuse in our inner cities? What is it about the way that I think that supports the continuing spread and decline of the ghetto? Why don't we have a national, state, county, and city coordinated set of goals to solve the problems in the ghettos? Why are we spending billions of dollars and untold man-hours on trying to control violence, drugs, crime, and so on, and almost nothing on helping people learn to reprogram themselves and chose not to engage in these activities?

The Simba corporation teaches children and adults to think differently about themselves, their circumstances, and their environment. We do not teach people *what* to think, but *how* to think. We give people back their power of choice—to take full responsibility for how they choose to think, feel, and act— and to learn how to achieve the results that they want in their lives, regardless of their circumstances. This is the only true form of empowerment, the only true ghetto solution.

Multi-culturalism. Be careful of this word. In many instances, it is the new racism. It is the new form of the master mentality and control. It sounds good to say, "We are going to have a multi-cultural program." But too often, what that turns out to be is one program for everybody. And that program is usually written or governed by white people and is a white perspective on the different cultures involved. This requires the participants to adopt white thinking patterns. So, believing that it is possible to have one program to fit all is as ridiculous as believing that one person can understand the experience of everyone else. It is not possible. Indeed, this multi-culturalisim, though more subtle than outright prejudice, is perhaps the most insidious form of racism today.

Today's racist completely negates the uniqueness of black people, and other cultures, by enacting policy and spending money as if there was no difference between white people and black people. It is so difficult to get white people, and some black people, to understand that they invalidate us by saying there is no difference. How would you like your lover to say, "Dear, I just want you to know that you are just like every other lover I ever had." This is the demeaning nature of multi-culturalism.

White Americans tend to have this either/or thinking

pattern—there is only one right answer, either yours or mine, so of course since I can't be wrong, I will make you *right* by making you just like me—instead of a both/and thinking pattern that realizes that there is an infinite number of possible answers, so you are OK and I am OK without our needing to be the same. Each of us experiences life uniquely. Even between two different people of the same culture, race, age, and sex, each individual could be presented with the same experience and each would interpret it in a totally different way.

But that doesn't mean that there aren't some common characteristics in this packaged group of thinking patterns called "culture." We should identify these common patterns and then approach individuals according to those patterns. Then, instead of having a *multi-cultural* approach—we have a *culturally specific* approach.

This is the approach we must adopt if we are going to be effective and not waste the billions of dollars we did in the sixties and seventies on urban renewal, model cities and wars on poverty. We need to understand what the truth of the matter is and move with it. And the truth is: we are what we think, and African American people living in our ghettos are quite capable of thinking for themselves and running their own affairs. And until we help people change how they *think*, we are not going to change how they *feel*, and we are not going to change how they *act*.

Now is the time for both/and thinking. Yes, we need reinvestment in our cities. Our cities need better healthcare, housing, jobs, police, fire services, and schools. And yes, the people need to be taught how to take responsibility for how they think, feel, and act towards themselves, their circumstances, and their environment. They need to learn not to choose to be a victim of their circumstances, the economy, politics, or political parties.

The "big lie" taught African Americans to see others as more powerful and more competent than themselves which gave them the excuse to blame others for their circumstances. Any time we blame, no matter how well deserved that blame is, we give away our power to act. *All blame must go.* When something is not productive in our lives or our community, the question is not, Whose fault is it? but, What must I do to change this?

Some people complain about Koreans, Asians, and Middle Easterners having successful businesses in ghetto communities. To blame these people for seeing the glass half-full and taking advantage of an entrepreneurial opportunity is to perpetuate and buy into the "big lie" that others are more competent and better able to work together than African Americans.

Black men and women do not understand this slavery-time programming has kept them complaining and blaming, but not acting to improve their situation. It is so important for us to understand that we were not immigrants. Our history, culture, and identity were destroyed, and we were reprogrammed in the master's house. Simba teaches people how to overcome this negative programming and choose more positive programming.

When we African Americans truly understand what has happened to us, then we will know what power really is. We are born with power—the ability to choose, to act, and to achieve. We are born with the power to define our own reality instead of letting others define it for us. We are born with the power to choose to see opportunity regardless of our circumstances. And we are born with the power to act to overcome those circumstances, and create for ourselves the lives we know in our hearts we deserve.

Any time we allow ourselves to blame any person, thing, or circumstance, we are choosing to be victims and we give our power away to that person, thing, or circumstance. As long as we believe that power is money and politics, we will be victims of our own thinking, waiting for someone with power to empower us, to change our lives for us. When we understand that we all have power of our own—the power to make choices and take action and achieve results—*only* then, will we truly be empowered—because no one else can do this, only we can choose to empower ourselves.

We are not descendants of slaves. We are descendants of a group of people who were enslaved. That's a big difference. Many of our slave forefathers and foremothers understood their power. When the Emancipation Proclamation was signed and slavery was legally abolished, our ancestors left those plantations with little or nothing. There was no welfare. No forty acres and a mule. No food stamps, and no emotional trauma transition teams.

As a matter of fact, what they faced was murder—white people liked to call it lynching, to give it kind of a legal connotation. They faced violence, racism, and prejudice unlike anything we know today. Yet look at what they did. They became land owners, business owners, they founded educational institutions, and became professionals, in spite of their circumstances.

They are probably looking down upon our people in the ghetto today saying, "You can go where you want to go when you want to go there. You can meet together publicly and form organizations to work together. You can pool your money and talent. You can buy what you want to buy without the approval of white people. You can ask your wealthier African American brothers and sisters to invest with you. You can even ask white people to invest with you. What are you waiting for? Look at what we did with so much less. Wake up our children, and realize who you really are and the power you really have."

In 1986/87 I began my research to develop a solution to our ghetto problems. One of the first problems I realized was the identity issue. I define identity as a feeling of uniqueness combined with a feeling of connectedness to a greater whole. African American people lack that feeling of connectedness to the greater whole of American society. That is why so many African American people straighten their hair and/or adopt the lifestyles of white people—so they can feel connected to a greater whole. Others get this feeling of connectedness by identifying with Africa. And some get this feeling by knowing they are spiritual beings living a human experience and identifying with God.

Culture is learned. If I took you out of your mother's womb at birth, took you to China and gave you to Chinese parents, today you would look pretty much as you look today, but you would speak Chinese, eat Chinese, your politics would be Chinese, your religion would be Chinese, you would think Chinese, and you would be Chinese. So you see, there really are no inherently white people, black people, Indian people, Asian people, Spanish people, Eskimo people, and so on. There are only people who group themselves together by similar belief systems and thinking patterns, and common experiences.

Because of this, if you look around the world today, you will see black Americans, black Russians, black Africans, black Englishmen, black Mexicans, black Indians, black Frenchmen, black Canadians, and so on, because they have the same thinking patterns and common experiences of their host culture.

Because being black is a secondary identity (Alvin F. Poussaint, M.D. and James P. Comer, M.D. discuss this in their wonderful book, *Raising Black Children*), I realized that our primary identity is to be an effective, emotional human being. After this is accomplished, then the person can better integrate their learned culture. This is a major part of what Simba accomplishes in its adult training, and what the adults then teach the children. The Simba Constitution exemplifies this.

Also, there is an underlying rage within African American people against white people for all of the atrocities that have occurred and are continuing to occur. This underlying rage is usually unspoken, except maybe in small groups, and may even be subconscious in some people. This rage is really never openly seen until you have a riot, but we visit it in many forms upon ourselves and upon society. The statistics in the appendix of this book clearly show the results of this rage, and of the dysfunction that has been caused by African Americans being nurtured and programmed in a white-American society. The solution to this dysfunction of African American people, especially in the ghettos, is to first recognize the rage and the pain caused by this dysfunction, then to use the power of choice to take responsibility for it, and finally, to use the power of action to vent those destructive energies in nondestructive ways to achieve the change we really want. Simba teaches adults and children how to do this.

It is important to understand that we must shift our focus off the child and onto the teacher or role model. As James Baldwin said, our children do not follow our words but our actions. Drs. Comer and Poussaint say, "...during infancy, the first two years of life, the infant must establish a relationship with a caretaker, which becomes a blueprint for future relationships with other people. It is now that the biological, social, and emotional patterns are established which, with modification, will remain with the infant for the rest of his or her life."

Joseph Chilton Pearce and Phylicia Rashad, authors of the

audio tape series, "The Complete Guide to Understanding Childhood," state "...It is important to recognize that ninety-five percent of all learning occurs beneath conscious awareness. As a result, children simply become like their models. Every child around you is going to unconsciously become who you are. Young children live in the emotions of their models, so there is no hiding your emotional state from a young child. That is why I suggest that we each become who we wish our children to become."

A child has many different teachers: peers, parents, relatives, school teachers, community people, media images, society, and others. Who teaches the child reared in a dysfunctional family and community how to identify with which models? One of our major mistakes is that we focus directly on the children—what are their grades? behavior?—and what we don't understand is that children are the result of someone else's modeling. So, by focusing on the children, we are not dealing with the cause of their programming. We are dealing with the children after they have been programmed, after they have the belief systems and the thought patterns instilled in them by adults.

So what we do in Simba is to focus first on the teacher or role model. What negative programs, belief systems, and thought patterns does the prospective mentor have? They come to us with lives that are not working well—with problems in relationships (with themselves, God, and others), with economic issues, with health issues, with self-expression issues, and many others. Then we help the mentor adjust those programs, belief systems, and thought patterns to help them achieve the results they want in their own lives, a process which they will in turn pass on to the child.

One time I was attending a youth conference on violence and abuse. An elderly, African American woman wearing black-lens sunglasses (indoors), a black, straight hair wig, a black dress, and a black coat stood and said that all we have to do to put an end to violent children is to change the laws so we can beat them more. Where did we ever get the idea that beating someone is the way to teach them not to be violent? Maybe this is something else that we learned from the master, who beat us regularly. Our children learn to use violence to solve their problems because adults use violence to solve their problems with children and other adults. We must love and nurture our children as the irreplaceable and precious beings they are, and then they will, in turn, learn to treat others that way also.

In addition to designing a program whose content is truly prevention-based, I have also created a unique implementation structure. When I first looked at the various programs providing services to the ghetto community, I discovered four primary barriers:

1. The programs were funding-dependent. When funds were cut, services to our youth stopped.

2. Volunteers generally served less than one year. So there was a lack of long-term consistency for our youth.

3. Volunteer training was minimal or non-existent, and was of dubious quality and effectiveness.

4. Most volunteers were Caucasian and culturally ineffective.

I eliminated these barriers within the structure and process of Simba, Inc.:

1. After the initial training cost, each Simba, Inc., chapter is financially independent.

2. Simba leaders commit to volunteer for twelve or more years.

3. All Simba leaders must successfully complete sixty-six hours of training.

4. All Simba leaders are African American and representative of the community they serve.

Life is always telling us when to make adjustments; the problem is that we choose not to listen. African Americans, less than 12 percent of the American population, are responsible for 64 percent of all robberies and 54 percent of all murders in the nation, and our national state prison population is 46 percent black, and only 33 percent white.

Our criminal justice system is staggering under its financial and human cost. Some court systems cannot afford to prosecute many criminal cases and some police departments can no longer make arrests for many crimes because there is no room and/or money to jail offenders.

And yet our response to this as a country is that instead of spending time, money, and effort on prevention, directly in the ghetto community, we will spend billions on more prisons, more police, more courts, more laws, more lawyers, and more of anything else we can think of that has already been tried and has already failed. We are struggling to maintain a standard of living in America while sacrificing our quality of life. We must let go of our instinct as a country to address the symptoms of our society's problems, instead of attacking the roots of the problems themselves. We must emphasize prevention before the fact, not incarceration after the fact.

And we are all paying the price for this—white, black, Chicano, Asian—everyone. No one is exempt. Not the homeless people in the streets, not the immigrant workers in the inner-cities, not the middle-class families in the suburbs, not the millionaires in their mansions, not even the politicians in their white-columned capitol buildings—we all pay a price.

I am reminded of a story about a group of explorers lost in the Amazon jungle of South America. They broke through the dense trees and underbrush and came into a clearing next to the wide, rushing Amazon river. The raging river was full of helpless men, women, and children being carried downstream to their deaths. At the river's edge, tents with large red crosses on them were set up and hundreds of helpers were pulling people out of the water. They managed to save many, but the river was too large and flowing too quickly, and many were lost. The director of the helpers pleaded with the leader of the explorers to stay and help them save more people. The leader refused and instead continued his journey upstream. When the explorers finally reached the mouth of the Amazon river, they halted, set up camp, and began to stop people from falling into the river.

Appendix

THE DEATH & DESTRUCTION
OF OUR CHILDREN

Every 4 hours a Black child is **murdered**.

Every 43 minutes a Black baby **dies**.

Every 6 hours a Black child **dies from a gunshot wound**.

Every 20 hours a Black child or young adult under 25 dies from causes related to **HIV (AIDS)**.

Every 46 seconds of the school day, a Black child **drops out of school**.

Every 65 seconds a Black teenager becomes **sexually active**.

Every 69 seconds a Black baby is born to an **unmarried mother**.

Every 95 seconds a Black baby is born into **poverty**.

Every 104 seconds a Black teenage girl **becomes pregnant**.

Every 3 minutes a Black baby is born to a mother who **did not graduate from high school**.

Every 6 minutes a Black baby is born at **low birth-weight**, weighing less than 5 pounds 8 ounces.

Every 7 minutes a Black baby is born to a mother who had **late or no prenatal care**.

Every 11 minutes a baby is born to a Black teen mother who **already had a previous child**.

Every 11 minutes a Black child is arrested for a **violent crime**.

Every 18 minutes a Black child is arrested for a **drug offense**.

Every 76 minutes a Black child is arrested for an **alcohol-related crime**.

SOURCE: Children's Defense Fund, Washington, D.C.

THE DEATH & DESTRUCTION
OF OUR PEOPLE

If current patterns continue, by the year 2,010, 75 percent of all African American youths will be in **jail or prison**.

African American males in America are incarcerated at a rate five times that of **South Africa**.

Out-Of-Wedlock births in 1950 for all African Americans was 16.8 percent and 1.7 percent for White Americans. In 1988, it was 63.7 percent for African Americans and 14.9 percent for White Americans. In 1960, 20 percent of all African American children were living in **fatherless families**, compared to 60 percent in 1993.

African Americans are 12 percent of the U.S. population, and in 1990 committed 53.9 percent of all **murders**, and in 1989, 63.9 percent of all **robberies**.

Homicide is the leading cause of death among African American males 15–24 years old. From 1978–1987, annual homicide rates for young African American males were 5–8 times higher than young white males.

In 1977, more African American males were **killed** by other African American males than during the entire nine year period of the Vietnam War.

The 1989, **risk of death from homicide by a gun** for African American males 15–19 years of age was 84.3 per 100,000 people compared with 7.5 for white males—or eleven times the risk.

For violent crimes that involve African Americans and whites in 1987, whites assault whites at about the chance-encounter rate, African Americans assault whites at about 72 percent of the chance-encounter rate, whites assault African Americans at about 56 percent of the chance-encounter rate, **but African Americans assault African Americans at 800 percent of the chance-encounter rate**.

In 1990, of those African Americans who were **alive at 65 years or older**, 61.6 percent were female and 38.4 percent were male.

African American teenagers were 38.2 percent of all **HIV (AIDS)** infections in 1992, and 71 percent of all infections were boys.

The percent of African American children living in **poverty** in 1991 was 44.1 compared to 11.4 for whites.

The **degrees in higher education** awarded to all African Americans in 1980 was 9,494 and in 1988, only 4,188. Only 13 percent of African Americans are college educated.

In the 1980's while the total **enrollment in higher education** grew by 12 percent, the enrollment of African American males decreased by 7.2 percent

In 1988, African American men had a 68 percent higher death rate from **heart disease**, 90 percent higher **stroke** rate, 71 percent higher **cancer** rate, 126 percent higher **liver** ailment rate, and an 86 percent higher **diabetes** rate than the total population. African American men younger than 45 years have a 45 percent higher rate of **lung cancer** and ten times the likelihood of dying from **hypertension** than whites.

SOURCE: *Civic Consultants, Chicago, Illinois & Two Nations, by Andrew Hacker.*

Simba, Inc. Constitution

PREAMBLE. We dedicate ourselves to empowering African Americans to choose their own greatness. Our life work is to help our people create more positive internal self-images, greater self-love and higher self-esteem. To trust ourselves and each other. To effectively set and achieve goals. To work together. To heal the pain of the past. To effectively deal with anger, fear, sadness, guilt and shame. To achieve and maintain life balance. To have successful man and woman and child and family relationships. To create our future independent of past limitations and current circumstances based on this truth: we already have everything we need, right now, to do whatever we choose to do. To make choices based on what we want rather than decisions based on what is available. To teach ourselves and our children to choose self-programming, and to be limitless in all aspects of living through faith, affirmations, visualizations and persistent action. To live knowing the truth that we are all spiritual beings living a human experience and that there is only one race on the planet earth: the human race.

OUR VISION. We see African American people achieving their greatness in Wealth, Health, Relationships and Self-Expression.

OUR GOAL. We empower a generation of African American people, one mind at a time, who will continue to empower each new generation, one mind at a time.

OUR ACTIVITY. We establish 5,000 Simbas in 50 states in the United States of America by January 1, 2000.

"We are all in a post-hypnotic trance induced in early infancy." Ronald Laing.

"We either make ourselves miserable or we make ourselves strong. The amount of work is the same." Don Juan, Journey To Xtlan.

"Education is our passport to the future, for tomorrow belongs to the people who prepare for it today." Malcolm X.

"A man who won't die for something is not fit to live." Martin Luther King, Jr.

"Truth is proper and beautiful in all times and in all places." Frederick Douglas.

"Go! As you believe so shall it be done unto you." Jesus Christ, Matt 8:13, Mark 11:22-24